These were men on fire with the love of God and eager to witness to the Gospel for the sake of the salvation of his people. What a legacy to inherit! What inspiring lives to emulate and imitate!

—The Most Reverend Alfred C. Hughes, archbishop emeritus of New Orleans

†

This inspiring story can seduce beyond the Catholic world: it resonates powerfully.... It is also a beautiful reminder that, even in dark times and dark places, human beings are spiritual beings who can sacrifice themselves for the common good and to imitate God's love. This historical episode is a needed message for our Western world, which lost this spiritual fighting spirit and the salvation of souls as the ultimate horizon.

—Tristan Casabianca, author

†

This is a story from the very heart of America, one of love and sacrifice in a time of darkness and desperation. When the last paragraph is finished, the reader will be left with the sadness that such remarkable men should have died so young but also with a strange feeling of warmth in the great strength, selflessness and faith that these five priests demonstrated.

—Alexander Mikaberidze, PhD, historian and author

SHREVEPORT MARTYRS OF 1873

THE SUREST PATH TO HEAVEN

Very Reverend Peter B. Mangum, JCL; W. Ryan Smith, MA;
Cheryl H. White, PhD

Foreword by Archbishop Christophe Pierre, Apostolic Nuncio to the United States

Published by The History Press
Charleston, SC
www.historypress.com

First published 2021

Manufactured in the United States

ISBN 9781467150903

Library of Congress Control Number: 2021943554

We offer you no salary, no recompense,
no holiday or pension.
But, much hard work, a poor dwelling,
few consolations, many disappointments,
frequent sickness, a violent or lonely death,
and an unknown grave.

—recruiting prospectus to French seminarians, Bishop Louis Dubourg of Louisiana and the Two Floridas (circa 1813)

This is dedicated to the memory of Father Isidore Quémerais, Father Jean Pierre, Father Jean Marie Biler, Father Louis Gergaud and Father François Le Vézouët, martyrs to the charity that immolates.

Contents

Foreword

When I arrived in Haiti twenty-five years ago to begin my ministry as official representative of the Holy Father to that country, I was happy to learn that Brittany, the western region of France where I was born, had sent more than eight hundred missionary priests to that small country since the end of the eighteenth century. These members of the Society of St. Jacques had given their whole lives to the proclamation of Christ's Good News. The beautiful church that I was privileged to serve was the fruit of their heroic efforts, as well as those of numerous other religious men and women, among whom were many who also came from Brittany.

I also discovered with great joy that Brittany had sent a good number of its priests and religious to North America at about the same time their counterparts were sent to Haiti. These missionaries all generously accepted the invitation of Bishop Auguste Marie Martin, who, like me, came from the Brittany town of Saint-Malo, to join him in the mission of evangelization in what was then his Diocese of Natchitoches, located in the northern part of Louisiana. The historic Diocese of Natchitoches is now the Dioceses of Alexandria and Shreveport.

Five of those priests did not hesitate to care for the hundreds of victims of the devastating yellow fever epidemic that occurred from August to November 1873 in Shreveport. They included Father Jean Pierre, Father Jean Marie Biler and Father François Le Vézouët from the Diocese of St. Brieuc et Tréguier; Father Isidore Armand Quémerais from the Archdiocese of Rennes; and Father Louis Marie Gergaud from the Diocese of Nantes.

These holy priests live on in the memory of the people not only because of their apostolic work in helping to build the Church in that part of Louisiana but, above all, because of their heroic sacrifices.

I am delighted that His Excellency Francis Malone, bishop of Shreveport, has taken the initiative to make known the beautiful Christian witness of these five martyrs of charity. During my recent visit to the Diocese of Shreveport, I had the opportunity to pray at their tombs, and I have observed firsthand the people's authentic devotion to these holy men. I am sure that the present detailed story, prepared by the Very Reverend Peter B. Mangum, Mr. William Ryan Smith and Dr. Cheryl White, will be a tremendous help to many people, as it has been to me, in discovering an amazing model of sanctity in these humble and dedicated men. The extraordinary context of their lives and deaths continues to captivate and inspire us.

This book, *Shreveport Martyrs of 1873: The Surest Path to Heaven*, is certainly a new contribution to the glorious story of the foundation of the Catholic Church in the United States of America. Given the challenges that we face in the current COVID-19 pandemic, I believe that the sacrifices of these giants in the faith have a special significance for our time. As a Frenchman and a fellow Brittany priest, I am particularly proud of them and of all who have chosen freely to leave their homeland in generous response to their missionary calling.

—Archbishop Christophe Pierre
Apostolic Nuncio
Washington, D.C., October 22, 2020

ACKNOWLEDGEMENTS

This book began as a conversation among three friends on pilgrimage in the Holy Land in May 2016. In a discussion of the martyrdom so evident in that sacred place, a Roman Catholic priest, an author of historical fiction and a university history professor together recalled the story, known to them all, of five priests who laid down their lives in the great yellow fever epidemic of 1873 in Shreveport, Louisiana. From that initial conversation, the intention to write a book took the form of a series of drafts over the next few years, each increasingly expanded, as research revealed ever more of the lives of these priests. Indeed, it was the primary research for this book that led us to realize that their lives were not only interesting but *exemplary models* of virtue. Each one, in his turn, willingly fell as a martyr to his charity: Father Isidore Quémerais, Father Jean Pierre, Father Jean Marie Biler, Father Louis Gergaud and Father François Le Vézouët.

This manuscript therefore formed the basis of petitioning the Vatican's Congregation for the Causes of Saints for the necessary *nihil obstat*, that a canonization inquiry might begin. By the formal act of Bishop Francis Malone of the Diocese of Shreveport on December 8, 2020, they are all officially now titled *Servants of God*, the first step in the canonization process.

The authors use the historical framework of 1873 Shreveport and the third-worst epidemic of yellow fever on record in the United States as background for highlighting the story of their heroic virtue. Written in a unique style that blends historical narrative with visionary descriptive prose, we believe this is a message perhaps especially appropriate for our current time but one that is also universal and eternal in its scope. This book provides what is a narrow abridgement of the fullness of their stories, and we have taken care to emphasize the choice each priest willingly made to die for others. There is much more to their lives than this volume can contain, making even this finished published work a mere beginning of making known their remarkable lives and deaths.

There are many people we wish to thank who made this project possible: Bishop Francis Malone of the Diocese of Shreveport and the Chancery of the Diocese of Shreveport. Also, Bishop Denis Moutel of the Diocese of St. Brieuc and Tregiuer, Auxiliary Bishop Alexandre Joly of the Archdiocese of Rennes and Bishop Jean Paul James, formerly bishop of Nantes, now archbishop of Bordeaux, for their research assistance, opening their archives and hospitality in welcoming our American delegation in February 2019. The descendants of the Quémerais and Le Vézouët families of Brittany have also been a great resource.

We extend a special warm thanks to Archbishop Christophe Pierre, Apostolic Nuncio to the United States, and a native of Saint-Malo, France. Archbishop Pierre has taken an enthusiastic interest in the stories of these five sons of Brittany and has been a champion of their cause. We are especially grateful for his foreword to this book.

We are grateful to the many other depositories of the rich Catholic heritage of this period of Louisiana history: University of Notre Dame Archives; the Archdiocese of New Orleans; the Jesuit Archives and Research Center in St. Louis, Missouri; Holy Trinity Church in Shreveport; St. Matthew's Church in Monroe, Louisiana; St. John the Baptist Church in Many, Louisiana; the Minor Basilica of the Immaculate Conception in Natchitoches, Louisiana; the Diocese of Alexandria, Louisiana; the Noel Archives and Special Collections of Louisiana State University at Shreveport; the Cammie G. Henry Research Center at Northwestern State University; and the Special Collections and Archives of University of Louisiana.

For those who reviewed and critiqued this work in progress, we offer a special thanks: Tristan Casabianca, Chantal Dickson, Martha Fitzgerald, Carol Gates, Dr. Gary Joiner, Dr. Alexander Mikaberidze, John Nickelson, Leslie Smith and Father Gregory Wilson. Thanks also to Lela Robichaux, graduate research assistant at Louisiana State University at Shreveport, and Margi Sirovatka.

For you, our readers, we hope you find inspiration and hope in these selfless priests.

INTRODUCTION

In 1852, the Roman Catholic bishops of the United States gathered at the Plenary Council of Baltimore and recommended the erection of a new diocese to cover the entire northern part of the state of Louisiana. There, pitiable resources hampered the growth of Catholicism, with a small but admirable cadre of émigré clerics and religious. The council established the Diocese of Natchitoches with the see city at the oldest permanent settlement in the Louisiana Purchase territory, the town of Natchitoches, founded in 1714. Farther south, the Catholic faithful rejoiced at the news of New Orleans elevated to a new archdiocese as of July 19, 1850. This conferred prestige, placing the international port city on par with its northern counterpart of St. Louis, itself elevated to an archdiocese just three years earlier.[1]

To serve as bishop of the newly established diocese, Archbishop Antoine Blanc of New Orleans nominated the pastor of Natchitoches, a native of Saint-Malo, France, Father Auguste Marie Martin.[2] Father Martin had been in Louisiana since 1846, long enough to have familiarity with the diverse culture and peoples of the region, as well as the many challenges they faced. These challenges included a malady common to the region, yellow fever, which Martin himself contracted in 1848.

At the time of Archbishop Blanc's nomination, Father Martin was serving in the important role as dean of that northern territory for the archbishop. As a vicar forane, Martin served "vicariously" in the place of the archbishop as the priest charged with missionary oversight of the expanding Catholic population, the care of sick clergy, clerical discipline and stewardship of diocesan property, among other duties. He knew the northern reaches of Louisiana well and had the respect of its population.

In Rome on July 29, 1853, His Holiness Pope Blessed Pius IX approved Martin's nomination with a formal Bull of Appointment. That same summer, Louisiana witnessed an epidemic of yellow fever of a previously unmatched ferocity. Within a few weeks, New Orleans lost nearly twelve thousand residents. This scale of that epidemic was closely matched, in Martin's lifetime, only by another major yellow fever epidemic he saw exactly twenty years later in Shreveport.

Doubtlessly recalling his own first missionary excitement in his native Brittany, one of the first acts of Martin's episcopate was to return there, seeking young men whom he could move to similar action. Archbishop Blanc agreed to administer the Diocese of Natchitoches in his absence, and Father James J. Duffo, SJ, of the New Orleans Province, who later assisted during the epidemic of 1873, arrived in Natchitoches to help in the northern parts of the diocese. Bishop Martin notified the bishops of Rennes, Nantes and St. Brieuc et Tréguier that he would be traveling there and asked permission to recruit any willing candidates from their seminaries.[3]

From the port of Le Havre on Saturday, October 21, 1854, Bishop Martin set sail for a return to Louisiana. With him were Fathers Jean Baptiste Avenard, Jules Janeau and Louis Gergaud from the Diocese of Nantes, already ordained priests. From the Diocese of St. Brieuc et Tréguier came Jean Pierre, François Le Vézouët and Mathurin Chapin. From the Archdiocese of Rennes were Jean Marie Beaulieu and Jean Baptiste Malassagne. The group arrived in New Orleans on December 5, the first Tuesday of Advent, after a forty-day ocean crossing. When they disembarked, they heard the ominous news of another outbreak of yellow fever that once again ravaged Louisiana.[4] It was a portent of things to come.

With unseasonably oppressive heat, the young recruits soon faced an uncharacteristically harsh drought. All of this was challenge enough, but this was also during a time when they were trying to learn the English language, continue their studies for ordination and adjust to cultural differences.[5]

On May 28, 1855, Bishop Martin ordained Jean Pierre to the subdiaconate, and on September 21, 1855, the bishop ordained both Pierre and Le Vézouët to the diaconate. The following day, Bishop Martin ordained Jean Pierre a priest, one week shy of his twenty-fourth birthday. Le Vézouët waited nearly eight more months for his priestly ordination day on Saturday, May 3, 1856.[6] On the same afternoon of his priestly

Bishop Auguste Marie Martin of the Diocese of Natchitoches. *Courtesy of the Diocese of Shreveport.*

ordination, Father Pierre received from Bishop Martin the news of his first appointment. Bishop Martin established a new parish of the Church of the Holy Apostles of St. Peter and St. Paul at Bayou Pierre, with Father Jean Pierre as its first pastor. Following the purchase of forty acres of land, Father Pierre supervised the construction of the church and a rectory and began a small adjacent cemetery. Soon, Bishop Martin charged Father

The Church of the Holy Apostles of St. Peter and St. Paul, established in 1856 by Father Jean Pierre in Bayou Pierre, Louisiana. *Courtesy of the Diocese of Shreveport.*

Pierre with yet another building project—that of a church for Shreveport, to be dedicated to the Holy Trinity.[7] Father Pierre's final destination was in sight.

November 1855 saw another day of joy for the now two-year-old diocese as a group of ten Daughters of the Cross from Tréguier, France, of the Diocese of Saint Brieuc et Tréguier, led by Mother Mary Hyacinth Le Conniat, arrived in New Orleans to meet with Bishop Martin and Archbishop Blanc. Upon the encouragement of Father Jean Pierre, the Daughters established a new convent and novitiate in 1866 on the site of the old Fairfield Plantation, three miles south of Shreveport. The move set into motion a sharing of ministry between clergy and religious sisters that proved to be quite fateful.

The Civil War brought more than an expected share of economic loss to Bishop Martin's diocese, to say nothing of the effects of food and medicine shortages on the civilian population. He decided another return to France was necessary to present the Society of the Propagation of the Faith with a report of his needs, as well as to recruit additional missionaries from Brittany.[8]

Before the war's end in the spring of 1865, Father François Le Vézouët offered the first Mass in Many, Louisiana, in a private home, the beginnings of what would become the parish of St. John the Baptist. Father Louis

Mother Mary Hyacinth Le Conniat. *Courtesy of the Diocese of Shreveport.*

Gergaud, now pastor at St. Matthew's Church in Monroe, successfully established missions at Homer, Columbia, Harrisonville and Woodville.[9]

Within its first decade, the Diocese of Natchitoches grew from five members of the clergy (including the bishop), seven churches, a convent and one academy to sixteen priests and bishop, seventeen churches with one further under construction, three chapels, thirty-two station churches, four convents, four "literary institutions for girls," five day schools and one college. The bishop reported thirty thousand Catholics in the 1860 census.[10]

On September 26, 1865, Bishop Martin gathered his priests in Natchitoches before leaving the United States and appointed Father Louis Gergaud as vicar forane. Bishop Martin then spent the next month readying for a journey to his native France, and on December 15, he addressed the General Council of the Society for the Propagation of the Faith in Paris. He received an increased allotment for the coming year to assist in the rebuilding of a war-ravaged diocese.[11]

Bishop Martin returned to his diocese in the spring of 1866 to find Reconstruction underway, supervised by the United States military. The Diocese of Natchitoches gradually recovered economically and spiritually, as Bishop Martin readied himself to attend an Ecumenical Council (the

Vatican Council) called by Pope Blessed Pius IX, first announced in 1867, and set to open its first session on December 8, 1869. The bishop saw the opportunity to once again visit Brittany to recruit more missionary priests.

In the early fall of 1869, Bishop Martin left New Orleans for New York, then on to the familiar port of Le Havre. From there, he once again visited the seminaries in Nantes and Rennes, where he conducted interviews with a dozen new potential recruits. On his return from Rome nearly a year later, he finalized a new cohort of young Bretons to come to Louisiana.[12]

The *Morning Star and Catholic Messenger* newspaper of New Orleans reported in its August 6, 1870 edition: "Bishop Martin has returned from Rome. His Lordship has recruited twelve ecclesiastics, all children of Catholic and faithful Brittany."[13] Among the Bretons destined for Louisiana were Father Jean Marie Biler of the Diocese of St. Brieuc et Tréguier and Father Isidore Quémerais of the Archdiocese of Rennes. Father Biler was appointed chaplain for the Daughters of the Cross at Fairfield, and Quémerais was to begin learning English.

Writing to the Society for the Propagation of the Faith in Paris in 1872, Martin praised his clergy, saying he might have failed in the mission field of Natchitoches due to the "fight against apathy…without priests, without Christian schools." Yet by 1872, he was humbled to acknowledge his gains, which he did not credit to himself but to the "conquering priests" he recruited from across France in the previous two decades.[14]

No one could have known then that of those missionary priests, five were to offer up their lives in Shreveport just months later, amid an epidemic of merciless proportions, for the selfless love of others.

What follows is their story.

The Surest Path to Heaven

I know that I am taking the surest and shortest path to heaven.
—François Le Vézouët, priest, martyr to his charity

Storefront of E.D. McKellar, Fever Ward 2, Shreveport Ember Friday, September 26, 1873

Commemoration of Saints Cyprian and Justina, martyrs

The screams of a man trapped in irreversible delirium echoed along Texas Street. The wailing traveled the filthy and mired ditches the length of Levee Street.[16] The late afternoon sun was fading, and so was Whitt McKellar, the son of a prominent local merchant. Whitt lay in pain on the upper floor of his family's grocery and dry goods store across from Shreveport's idle steamboat landing.[17]

While his family had fled to high ground away from the pestilence enveloping Shreveport, Whitt assumed the role he was dealt in life, that of the firstborn son. Too young for the last war, at twenty-one years of age, he remained to tend the family enterprise. He guarded the commodities from thieves preying upon the stricken city.[18] Whitt was armed against robbers but defenseless against a sickness that infected him through a transmission no one yet understood.

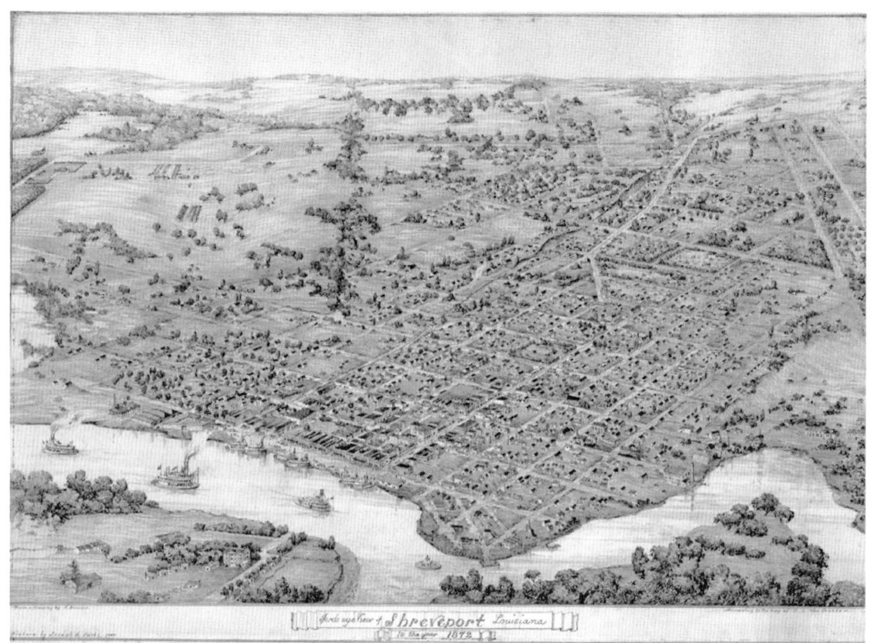

Bird's-eye view of Shreveport, 1872, drawn by H. Brosius. *Library of Congress Prints and Photographs Division, Washington, D.C.*

Death would not pass over him. The sounds of his anguish may have been lessened only by a brief rain shower that pelted the roofs of the commercial district, rattling the windowpanes of empty storefronts. The rain fell with the tears of many: the newlywed-turned-widow, the judge watching his family die, the mother caressing her lifeless infant and French nuns grasping their rosary beads in the convent's infirmary, pleading for a miracle to save their chaplain that very day. In this place where youth and promise were traded to safeguard material possessions sold for pennies of profit, the rain would, in a matter of days, reinvigorate the terrible yellow fever "tempest of death" that was strangling those who had dared to stay.[19]

The rain also fell three miles south of town at the St. Vincent Motherhouse, Novitiate and Academy for Girls, where their chaplain, Father Jean Marie Biler, was but a few hours from the same fate of young Whitt McKellar. Although dying, Father Biler had the consolation of the sisters from his native Brittany. Different from the lonely death facing young Whitt, Father Biler had kept his own deep faith.[20] The Last Rites would be for him a spiritual rampart for the journey from this life to the next. He had offered the same extreme unction to his *confreres* on their journey but ten days prior.

St. Vincent's Academy and Convent of the Daughters of the Cross, undated photograph from early twentieth century. *Image from Louisiana Digital Library.*

The sisters' consolation sought through the intercession of the day's saints—early fourth-century martyrs Cyprian and Justina—came when comparing that morning's Gospel passage and their chaplain's faith: "Whosoever shall confess me before men, him shall the Son of man also confess before the angels of God."[21] The thirty-three-year-old Father Biler, like the young businessman on Texas Street, would not survive the epidemic, and he had not denied his Lord. The heroic priest, a selfless foreign missionary, would not be moved again until after the rain had stopped, his body taken away for a proper Catholic burial.[22]

†

The Right Reverend Auguste Marie Martin waited at his Natchitoches residence, certainly watching the streets for the silhouette of Father François Le Vézouët. He had received communications from Shreveport, including a short and resolute dispatch that arrived a few days prior, a week before the rain shower fell there.

The priest he awaited was among his first recruits, serving as director of the Propagation of the Faith and a member of his bishop's council. Would Father Le Vézouët return in time to render aid? Would he have the courage to go to Shreveport? If he did, should the bishop even allow him to go? Whom else could he send?[23]

Father Le Vézouët arrived that evening with the hot Louisiana sun glowing red behind him. He was familiar with the route, as he traveled it often to teach in the seminary in Natchitoches he helped establish and to offer counsel to the bishop. In Many, just two years before, he had built a parish church dedicated to St. John the Baptist. It was there, beginning in 1865, between the Red River and the Sabine, in the deep woods and along the back-swamps—where the impoverished Creoles, Mestizos and indigent Spanish descendants subsisted—that the young French émigré priest spent most of his time. It was with the forgotten people that Father Le Vézouët's heart resided.[24]

When Father Le Vézouët arrived to the Natchitoches Cathedral of the Immaculate Conception, just one block from an old dead channel of the Red River, he met his bishop, who wasted no time in handing him the papers, which the priest unfolded and examined.[25] One was a desperate letter scrawled by Mother Mary Hyacinth, who feared Shreveport would soon be without the sacraments. Further, she reported that Shreveport's pastor and his assistant had succumbed to yellow fever just a few days earlier and that the remaining priest, a relative of hers, was deadly sick. The second

Seminary at Natchitoches, Louisiana, established by Bishop Martin. *Authors' collection.*

note was from Father Jean Marie Biler himself, requesting immediate aid, as everyone feared he would not live. Father Biler also sent a similar pleading missive to Father Louis Gergaud in Monroe.

According to the account of Bishop Martin, Father Le Vézouët read the communications in silence. "What would you like to do, my son?" Bishop Martin asked.

"Monseigneur, if you tell me to leave, I leave. If you leave it up to me, I stay."[26]

Bishop Martin paused, trying to understand "the real meaning of his words." More crowded silence grew between the men, holiness filled the void, until Father Le Vézouët added, "I want to go so much…" Then he paused again. "Monseigneur, if you left the decision up to me I would believe that in going I was acting according to my own will. I do not want to do anything but the will of God."[27]

Bishop Martin was leveled by the piety before him. He told the priest to make ready to go in relief of Shreveport.

The bishop did not need this to be one of the three-day sets of Embers Days[28] for him to intensify his prayer. This was the third set of four in the Church calendar, tied to the seasonal cycles of farming and harvesting. Christians since the first centuries had used these days of prayer, fasting and abstinence to render thanks to God for the gifts of creation. Everyone knew the harsh historical lessons of yellow fever in epidemics past, and a frost would bring immediate relief, which was surely also a constant and fervent prayer.

The early Mass that Ember Saturday commemorated St. Eustace and companions, martyrs of the second century. Father Le Vézouët and Bishop Martin each celebrated private Mass and prayed the Collect: "O God, who granted us the grace to celebrate the birthday of Your blessed martyrs Eustace and companions, grant that we may also share their eternal happiness in heaven."[29] They knew that St. Eustace was one of the Fourteen Holy Helpers who, as a group and as individuals, were invoked when the Black Plague devastated Europe in the mid-fourteenth century and in times of epidemics since. The bishop and his protégé knew well the history of Brittany and the many plagues it had endured.

After Mass, Father Le Vézouët set his affairs in order and visited a few families in town. He prepared to depart, but only after the next morning's Mass of the Sixteenth Sunday after the Pentecost, on the Feast of St. Matthew, apostle, evangelist and martyr. As if recalling the heroism of St. Eustace and the Fourteen Holy Helpers the day before was not providential enough, the

Sunday Mass at the cathedral confirmed the holy decision already made, as the Gospel reading recounted Matthew's leaving his tax collector's post immediately upon Jesus's call to follow Him. Word of Father Le Vézouët's departure for Shreveport traveled quickly throughout the old Creole town. The concerned faithful approached him as he was preparing to leave.

"You are going to your death," someone spoke out among them.

"I believe it," Father Le Vézouët replied. Then, turning to face them directly, he said, "But I know that I am taking the surest and shortest path to heaven."[30]

The route to Shreveport was 110 miles of winding backwoods traces and rutted stage lanes. The dense pine forest, often bereft of human habitation due to poor soil and long stretches of limited fresh water, provided a stark contrast to the land of his birth. Five thousand miles away, in western France and less than a half day's journey on foot from the ocean, the village of Brélidy of the Diocese of Saint-Brieuc et Tréguier is also remote but lush and fertile. There, his family held ancient estates of rolling farmland. The landed family produced a gifted son who exhibited great faith and devotion early in life. Such was not always common in post-Revolutionary France. In his devotion, he likely prayed to the village patron St. Columba, before the bust statue containing his relic. Just as centuries before St. Columba discerned his call to leave his native Ireland for the desolate unknown of the Scottish isles, so young François would discern a similar call to leave his home. With his own love of learning, Father Le Vézouët mirrored his town's patron, with the same spiritual gift of teaching and inspiring others.[31] Father Le Vézouët, now with thoughts of his homeland second to those of his mission, traveled on horseback through the northern Louisiana pine forest, a lone traveler to his final destination.

Early in the evening of September 26, close to Shreveport, Father Le Vézouët headed to the Fairfield convent, where Mother Hyacinth had penned her desperate letter to the bishop on September 18.[32] In Brélidy, he would have to bow slightly to enter the low, chiseled rock archway into his family's medieval stone farmhouse. In Fairfield, the priest could walk upright through the convent's high-framed doorway without hesitation. Inside, he found Father Jean Marie Biler from Plourivo in the same Diocese of Saint-Brieuc et Tréguier, just hours from death, surrounded by the remaining sisters. At the entrance of the weary traveler, Father Biler, who had anointed both of Shreveport's now deceased priests, stirred in haste from delirium. "A peace which nothing could alter took possession

Parish church dedicated to St. Columba in Brélidy, France. *Authors' collection.*

The picturesque coastline of Brittany, France, at Plouézec, just northeast of Brélidy, the hometown of Father Francois Le Vézouët. *Authors' collection.*

of his soul" when Father Le Vézouët, without delay, gave "the consolations of the Church to his worthy confrere"[33]—the very sacramental act and consolation he was destined to repeat often in the coming days.

Father Biler, with full consciousness just before death, formally transferred his spiritual and temporal affairs to Father Le Vézouët. The afflicted priest began speaking again to his fellow Breton, repeating the same joyful expression in three of the four languages they both knew: English, French and Breton.

"I am going to Heaven! *Je vais au Ciel! Chan d'or Baradoz!*"[34]

Father Le Vézouët watched as the pious priest slipped away, entering "into a calm, a peace so that nothing disturbed him up until his last breath." After nine years as a priest and two years and eight months' service at St. Vincent's, thirty-three-year-old Father Jean Marie Biler was buried in the convent cemetery with the *ecclesia triumphans*, the fallen Daughters of the Cross.[35]

At Every Corner

If there is a city of the population of this in a civilized country that is filthier, and that furnishes at every corner a great variety of bad smells, we should like to hear of it.
—Daily Shreveport Times, *August 30, 1873*

Off New Orleans, Mississippi River Channel
Tuesday, June 24, 1873
Solemnity of the Nativity of St. John the Baptist

The 989-ton Spanish barque *Valparaiso* anchored in the opaque waters of the Mississippi River. *Valparaiso* and its crew waited below the old Creole capital to begin a precautionary and mandatory trade quarantine. The vessel had sailed from the port of Havana, Cuba, under ballast, carrying only vats of water and some stones along the spine of its keel to enhance stability in the choppy gulf crossing. Following nine days at sea with an otherwise empty hull, *Valparaiso* and its crew spent two further days in the preventative isolation.[36] It was normal for seaworthy vessels to queue down the river until receiving permission to dock. Port authorities ordered the vessel fumigated with burning clouds of chlorine in the cabin, quarters and between the decks. Carbolic acid was introduced into the bilge pumps and mixed into the stagnant water stored in the merchantman's hold. Cuba was known for exporting communicable tropical diseases. Such was the cost of commercial enterprise.[37]

Following the fumigation, the port authorities waved *Valparaiso* out of quarantine. The towboat *Ocean* pulled it upstream to the wharf on Thursday, June 26, and into the bustling heart of the Crescent City. The crew dispersed, and the vessel remained idle in the river at the head of Third Street in front of the newer American neighborhood, as the agents of the export firm M. Puig & Co. considered what to load onto the *Valparaiso*. Then, the nineteen-year-old first mate, José Maria Arua, native of Barcelona, began to show symptoms of a tropical illness and was taken to a friend's house in Marigny to recover. On July 8, Arua was dead.[38]

News of Arua's demise spread quickly. Wary eyes turned toward the steamer chimneys and masts of the ship-rigged traders. Thereafter, other vessels, including the steamers *C.H. Durfee*, *Belle Lee* and *W.S. Pike*, reported fever cases. The people of New Orleans knew this malady well, and the ordeal on the *Valparaiso* was far from over. Immediately following the first mate's death, the vessel was pulled away from port and again fumigated. As the deaths mounted, port authorities wrapped *Valparaiso* in noxious vapors every night for weeks on end and ensured that the entire crew gathered up and boiled their clothing. The deceased Arua's possessions, however, were burned in the street, as were the very bed and bedding on which he died. Public officials treated the neighborhood of his death with carbolic acid. For the remainder of July, fever spread, reaching the sections of "the city contiguous to the landing and track of the Mississippi River steamboats" plying the river. By the end of the season, more than two hundred people were dead along the New Orleans riverfront.[39] "Yellow Jack" was at hand.

New Orleans was no stranger to disease outbreaks. The city's origins as a major commercial center just above the sinuous mouth of the Mississippi River, situated in what French explorer Jean-Baptiste Le Moyne, Sieur de Bienville, termed "a beautiful crescent," meant it was destined to be the major urban population center west of the Appalachian Mountains. Its population was dense, transient and international—with no sustained and manageable check on the influx of immigrants and visitors. All of these characteristics contributed to a history laden with the annual opportunity for any number of illnesses. Although the city entombed many each fever season, still more people stepped ashore.

Despite these frequent dances with death, progress was not denied, and New Orleans inevitably influenced the growth of a small river port near Texas on the American frontier. Many goods were shared up and down the Mississippi River and along the connecting rivers. Religion, however, was not one of those easily transported commodities. The city of New Orleans and environs claimed a large Roman Catholic population (of French, African, German and Spanish descent). Yet with only some notable exceptions, north Louisiana remained heavily Anglo-Protestant. Even so, by the mid-nineteenth century, northern Louisiana was also home to a large Jewish population, with many families fleeing central and eastern Europe because of religious persecutions.

From New Orleans, cargo vessels increasingly turned northwest. In the summer of 1873, sustained steamer traffic churned its way up the Red River, though its channel was at times quite "narrow and snaggy."[40] The destination was Shreveport, along with a handful of dependent towns in the river valley. Shreveport was emerging in the new decade as a busy port—rising from relative obscurity to become an important commercial waypoint on the road to the American West.

Perhaps even more than New Orleans, Shreveport existed for the reception and distribution of river-borne goods. Louisiana was the first state to enter the Union after President Thomas Jefferson acquired the Louisiana Purchase territory in 1803. By the 1830s, Texas had become an independent republic, and speculators recognized the commercial opportunities of its neighboring Louisiana. In the upper stretches of the Red River, however, there was a significant challenge in the form of a logjam hindering navigation. Convinced of the river's importance, the U.S. Congress appropriated funding for a remedy in 1828.[41]

In 1836, investors acquired land from the Caddo nation and formed the Shreve Town Company (renamed Shreveport in 1839), bearing the surname of one of its founding members, Captain Henry Miller Shreve.[42] It was Shreve's work with the United States Army Corps of Engineers that had first cleared the "Great Raft." The rivercraft that Shreve chose to first pass through the Red River was the *Enterprise*, which certainly illustrates the ultimate objective of his work.[43]

At the time of his appointment, Captain Shreve was the superintendent of western waters, and lest his rank deceive, his previous service had been as a steamboat captain. Because he held many patents on snagboats for debris removal, and because he had successfully accomplished similar jobs before, he was a natural choice. Originally, the Corps of Engineers hoped to bypass the majority of the blockage by digging canals, but Shreve ultimately cut a fresh channel straight through it, forging a navigable river through American grit and determination.[44]

The completion of Shreve's project meant the northern portion of the Red River Valley was open for business. Riverboats moved from New

Orleans to the very doorstep of northeast Texas, a mere twenty miles from Shreveport, in just a matter of days. At the former trading post,[45] purveyors laid out an ambitious sixty-four-block grid along the banks of the Red River. The townscape was bounded on the north by Cross Bayou, east by the river itself, south by a back-swamp generously called Silver Lake and west by a seemingly endless pine forest stretching to Texas.

Its growing and dense population, transient traffic, humid climate, stagnant water and abundant mosquitoes provided the recipe for the spread of the little-understood but often devastating disease yellow fever. The first recorded outbreak in Shreveport in 1837 claimed the life of William Bennett, among the first permanent settlers. Nonetheless, optimism prevailed throughout the formative years, and as early as 1838, a correspondent with the *New Orleans Weekly Picayune* wrote:

> [Shreveport is] *a great thoroughfare for travelers to and from* [the Texas] *Republic....Light draught steamboats can reach the place all the year round....The town is improving fast. Eight new frame buildings are going up, including a large and spacious hotel. The settlers are remarkable for industry, intelligence and enterprise.*[46]

By 1850, Shreveport had a population of 1,700. Boardinghouses were hastily erected to accommodate the influx of people. In fact, many ordinary houses held non-family boarders, such was the shortage of residential accommodations.[47] Although land was plentiful, people were generally living in unusually dense proximity by American standards. The city attracted many immigrants, and the next decade saw a remarkable doubling of the population.[48]

Unlike much of the agrarian South, nearly a quarter of employed residents worked in commercial enterprise, including as cotton brokers, grocery clerks, retail merchants and hardware store owners.[49] Commercial entrepreneurs made their presence known, and by the time of the Civil War, Shreveport exhibited a uniqueness, "eminently cosmopolitan in... character, being made up of people from every state in the Union and from all nations of Europe."[50]

Although some areas were topographically well-suited for efficient drainage, a city grading project begun in the 1850s remained half-completed for want of funds and effective municipal leadership. In many localities, the natural drainage of the high areas toward the river, Cross Bayou and Silver Lake were diverted and leveled, without the requisite

Red River Raft, 1873. *Image by R.B. Talfor, Library of Congress Prints and Photographs Collection, Washington, D.C.*

drains added. The result was that "a rain of a few hours convert[ed] the town into a morass."[51]

Further, the public sewerage system was also incomplete. The "sewerage was so defective that the refuse of the hotels and boarding houses was [simply] poured out upon the surface of the ground" for easier disposal.[52]

> *As early as January* [1873] *the accumulated filth in the alleys of the city began to be oppressively offensive....Furthermore; the most public thourough-fares* [sic] *of the city were totally neglected; stagnant water, rotten garbage, animal excrement, filled the gutters; the refuse of hotels and boarding houses in every portion of the city poured out of private sewers, into the streets, there with dead cats, dogs, and rats to fester and emit the most noisome stench.*[53]

The summer of 1873 was a wet one, and the streets were "neglected and uncleaned; stagnant water, rotten garbage and animal excrement filled the gutters....The whole city [was] enveloped in a disgusting odor, from midnight to day."[54] "A sanitary police is unknown, and the only scavengers are hogs, which roam the streets at will, turning them into cess-pools."[55]

An original 1860s-era cistern inside the medical office building of Dr. Joseph Moore in Shreveport, Louisiana. *Authors' collection.*

Blame for the deplorable state of public health was routinely laid at the foot of the municipal government.[56]

There was no public supply of drinking water. Wells were not feasible so close to the Red River. The only reliable source of fresh water was found at Currie's Spring.[57] Water purchased from this spring cost five cents per bucket, which kept the poor away. Instead, most collected rainwater in massive cypress and brick storage cisterns. Little did anyone know that these were breeding grounds for the mosquito carrier of yellow fever.[58]

MUCH SICKNESS MAY RESULT

Just below the railroad landing lays the wreck of the steamer Ruby. *On and around her are fifty head of drowned cattle in all stages of decomposition sending forth a stench sufficient to engender a pestilence.... There is no telling how much sickness may result.*

—Daily Shreveport Times, *August 30, 1873*

RIVERFRONT, SHREVEPORT
TUESDAY, AUGUST 12, 1873
THE MEMORIAL OF ST. CLARE, VIRGIN

By the time Newton Walker closed his store's books for the evening, the temperature was still in the mid-eighties. Though he owned a simple shop, it was in a prime location across the street from the riverbank on the corner of Crockett and Levee Streets. Close to the principal steamboat landing, Walker had expected his store to yield great success.[59] The local newspaper carried lengthy editorials on the promising commercial future of Shreveport with the opening of the Texas and Pacific Railroad, predicting great crowds visiting the next day for a celebration of progress, with an appeal to the merchants to invite visitors into their stores—and even into their homes. Shreveport's hotels were already filled. Merchants could not leave the customers without a bed, or meal, in "reproach to our hospitality," nor leave them prey to hunger and mosquitoes.[60] Still, it was all too late for Walker. His business enterprise had already failed.[61]

Before the height of the dry season exposed numerous snags in the shallows of the Red River, shipments arrived and departed daily. Earlier that very day, a new steamer arrived with goods from New Orleans and beyond and deposited a fresh set of potential customers, but their purchases came too late to make a difference for Walker. After he closed his shop, he probably walked to a nearby boardinghouse, one of many, that catered to the transient laborers.[62]

Walker was ill but traveled the nearly three-mile southward trek along Bayou Pierre to his brother's house. There, he suffered for five days before a physician called on the house. Diagnosed with "yellow jaundice," the failed merchant recovered shortly thereafter. Yet two of the Walker children showed signs of a sudden and debilitating fever as Newton prepared to return to town. Within a matter of weeks, his brother's entire family was sickened. When Newton greeted his brother late in the evening of August 12, he had unwittingly cast a death sentence on the family. Five of them perished.[63]

Father Pierre and his assistant, the young Father Quémerais, greeted parishioners and visitors after the early morning Mass in honor of the Assumption of the Blessed Virgin Mary. Father Jean Pierre was the parish priest of the town's lone Roman Catholic church, Holy Trinity Church. The French missionary had a full head of hair coiffed in the fashion of the day—oiled, neatly parted and heavy over the ears—a broad smile and penetrating, sure eyes.

Father Isidore Quémerais likely saw not only the young family of the child he had baptized the previous Sunday but also the newlyweds whose Nuptial Mass he had performed on the first of May. This was his first wedding at Holy Trinity since he arrived the spring of 1873 and one of the very few weddings in his two years as a priest.

He certainly remembered his first baptism in Shreveport, on Passion Sunday, March 30, of that same year—that of the infant Francis John Flanagan. Francis was not expected to live long after birth, so he was baptized privately and quickly but without the solemnities of a Catholic baptism. The infant's parents, Thomas and Anna, later proudly brought him into the church where they met the new assistant priest who would "supply the ceremonies" for him. There would be no need to baptize him again, but all the rituals that normally surround a baptism were then performed.

Father Jean Pierre. *Courtesy of the Diocese of Alexandria, Louisiana.*

Father Quémerais met the family and godparents at the front of the church. He traced the sign of the cross on the infant's forehead and placed his first taste of blessed food in the form of salt praying for God to bestow upon him wisdom and eternal life. He invited them all to enter the wood-framed structure and brought them to the baptismal font, where he prayed the prayer of exorcism. He blessed the child's mouth and nostrils, and then, turning to Andrew Currie, the godfather, and Theresa Nolan, the godmother, he listened as, on behalf of their godchild, they renounced sin and professed the Catholic faith. Father Quémerais dipped his thumb into the Oil of Catechumens and anointed the child's breast in the sign of the cross. Since there was to be no baptizing with water, Father dipped his thumb into the fragrant Sacred Chrism, blessing the crown of Francis's head. The ceremonies were fully supplied once Francis John received the white garment and the candle lit from the Pascal Candle.

Such was the rhythm of Catholic life in Shreveport.

Meanwhile, that Friday and through the weekend, some riverboat crewmen and other strangers made their way to the Market Street Infirmary at Market and Travis Streets, just two blocks from the riverfront and steps from Holy Trinity Church. There, in the medical offices of Drs. Darwin Thornton Fenner, Thomas G. Allen and William Henry Williams, the strangers were diagnosed with "remittent fever."[64] The doctors compared these manifestations with symptoms Newton Walker had exhibited.[65] It was the high fever season, and the town had already seen its share of disease in its short history.[66]

The physicians recognized that an outbreak among the steamboat men would spread quickly, without knowing why. Further complicating the situation, several captains were taking advantage of the high water as they lined their riverboats along the upper and lower landings on the Red River. Among the line of steamers waiting idle was the *Ruby*. It lay tied up south of town with its crew making repairs and building cowpens while awaiting a load of cattle for the New Orleans market.[67] Despite the odor, Shreveport's dank streets were awash with inactive steamboat men and visitors celebrating the completion of the grand westward-reaching railroad.

Dr. Fenner, the physician who had treated Newton Walker, soon acknowledged that a member of his family was ill with fever. Next, a neighbor reported two more fever cases in the residence across the street from the infirmary. The tally of cases quickly rose. The troubling news was difficult to contain as the physicians began to argue the extent of what was wrong in Shreveport.[68]

At St. Vincent's just south of town, the routine of convent life continued. The sisters' attention that Saturday after the Feast of the Assumption was on celebrating the name day of their Superior, Mother Mary Hyacinth. Mother had done much to spread devotion to her patron, St. Hyacinth. The newly erected church in Moreauville, Avoyelles Parish, where the first convent of the Daughters of the Cross was located in the United States, was dedicated to St. Hyacinth.[69] When Father Louis Gergaud, the founding pastor of St. Matthew Church in Monroe, appealed for her help establishing a Catholic school, she yielded. Father Gergaud transformed his own residence into a new school in February 1866, and thus was born St. Hyacinth's Academy for Girls.[70]

On this day, Father Biler offered Mass with the sisters and mother superior in their chapel on beautiful manicured grounds. Father Biler had an easy Gospel passage on which to expound: the parable of the vigilant and faithful servants awaiting the return of their master from a wedding. "You also must be ready, because at an hour that you do not expect, the Son of Man is coming."[71] As they joyfully celebrated that saint's day within the octave of the Assumption, they could not have known the extent of the illness nearby.

By the beginning of the week, the Market Street Infirmary had no choice but to turn patients away, even if they were able to pay the minimum charge of five dollars per day. [72] On the evening of August 19, three more strangers staggered in, but together they were turned out to await their fate in the open air.[73] The editors of the *Daily Shreveport Times*, meanwhile, commented on a merciful respite from the searing heat.[74]

The weather may have been pleasant, but the cool morning light brought a formidable sight. Two of the strangers turned away from the infirmary were found dead in a street gutter near the front of the Mechanic's Exchange building at 35 Texas Street. The chief of police happened upon the missing third stranger, unconscious, still seated, trousers dropped, in the outhouse behind the building. Although the chief found a "quick, weak pulse," the man died en route to the very infirmary that had turned him away the night before.[75] The malady, which locals now dubbed "the

Stranger's Disease," was spreading, with more deaths recorded. The work at the Market Street Infirmary continued as the weather remained unseasonably, and deceptively, cool.[76]

Lieutenant Eugene Augustus Woodruff. *Courtesy of Noel Archives and Special Collections, Louisiana State University at Shreveport.*

Body-strewn gutters aside, the demands of the commercial market continued. That Thursday, August 21, six river packets were busy along the riverfront. Some of the vessels arrived at the muddy riverbank before Levee Street to unload manufactured wares and dry goods. Others departed from Shreveport with loads of cattle, cotton and passengers.[77] Only one merchant steamer remained idle: *Ruby*. It was beginning to bear the brunt of a snickering joke as "busy as a bee doing nothing."[78]

Meanwhile, upriver from *Ruby*, a few miles due north of the Mechanic's Exchange Building, United States Army Corps of Engineers lieutenant Eugene Augustus Woodruff, his brother George and their snagboat *Aid* worked in the steamy heat clearing logjams and crafting elaborate elevation drawings of the environs of the river. The sunken trees were pulled up only with great effort. When they would not budge, the crew used explosives, evidenced by columns of red water leaping into the air. This was assurance that commercial interests would continue.[79]

Woodruff sketched masterful charts and captured still images of the work at hand. Technology, northern ingenuity and southern muscle cleared the river again. Keeping the river navigable had proven a considerable challenge, and the Corps of Engineers wasted no time in sending a contingent of men to keep commerce steady.[80]

Woodruff and his crew knew their efforts were effective.[81] The plying steamboats and the Texas and Pacific Railroad—the "great future highway of the nation"—kept the community in a flurry of activity.[82] However, the boardinghouses lining Texas Street were inundated with fever cases.[83] Local authorities publicly downplayed the growing evidence for alarm as nothing more than a series of unfortunate coincidences.

August 24 commemorated the Feast of St. Bartholomew, apostle and martyr, flayed alive. As the date fell on Sunday in 1873, the readings and prayers proper to the day were replaced by those for the Twelfth Sunday

The snagboat *Aid* on the Red River in 1873. *Library of Congress Prints and Photographs Collection, Washington, D.C.*

after Pentecost. Within the whitewashed walls of Holy Trinity Church, minds and hearts were filled with hope at the preaching of their pastor on the healing that Jesus performed for crowds of people:

> *A great crowd of his disciples and a large number of the people…came to hear Him and to be healed of their diseases; and even those who were tormented by unclean spirits were cured. Everyone in the crowd sought to touch Him because power came forth from Him and healed them all.*[84]

The same day, a broadside advertisement appeared in the *Times* announcing the arrival of the Great James Robinson's Circus. "The great show of the south" was enthusiastically received. The circus camped on the corner of Edwards and Milam Streets in the very heart of town. Its arrival brought still more travelers, with promises of more than 150 equestrian performers in tow and numerous other oddities. The circus was set to perform the upcoming Saturday morning of August 30.[85]

By August 25, there were so many cases of fever that doctors were unable to handle the workload. Rather than excitement for an "exposition of

ON SATURDAY, AUGUST 30,

WILL THE

"GREATEST SHOW ON EARTH"

EXHIBIT IN THE CITY OF SHREVEPORT!

AWAIT THE ADVENT OF THE RELIABLE!!

THE GREAT AND ONLY ROBINSON EQUESTRIAN IS COMING!!

DO NOT BE AGAIN DECEIVED BY THE PRETENTIOUS DISPLAY OF CHARLATAN INSTITUTIONS!

On account of the liberal patronage everywhere accorded to the

Great Show of the South! America's Exposition of Wonders!

—AND—

THE GREAT JAMES ROBINSON'S CIRCUS,

And to prevent the masses from being deceived by false representations of pretentious adventurers, the Management have arranged for their

MAMMOTH CONSOLIDATION

TO EXHIBIT THROUGHOUT THE SOUTH MUCH EARLIER THAN ANTICIPATED AND HAVE THEREFORE DECIDED TO EXHIBIT AT

SHREVEPORT, SATURDAY AUGUST 30

Advertisement from the *Daily Shreveport Times*, August 24, 1873.

wonders" set to open, panic ensued as the fever spread to the ranks of the wealthier citizens. By the end of August, at least twenty-nine Shreveporters had perished, and many more were very sick.[86]

Late Wednesday afternoon, August 27, the crew of the perpetually idle steamboat *Ruby*—still the subject of ridicule throughout the town—at last began to take on its load of 182 head of cattle. What it lacked in timeliness, it would make up for in gross product. The crew prepared for a belated evening departure to the New Orleans market, having been moored more than a week along the riverbank, with the newly formed cowpens on deck.[87]

As the last of the cattle were loaded, something frightened the herd. Such a commotion ensued that *Ruby* was nearly ripped apart as the cattle dashed about. Nearly half of the cattle stampeded off the *Ruby*, crashing into the mud of the riverbank and the wooded landscape beyond. The sudden sprint of cattle left many others tied inside the pens along the starboard side, resulting in a near total capsizing of the vessel. When the *Ruby* finally stopped thrashing in the channel, it sank into the river to its upper works, a perfect wreck in the riverbed. About half of the cattle were lost, with dozens drowned in the twisted timber works.[88]

As the *Ruby* settled into the muck, a chambermaid from the *C.H. Durfee* named Nancy took gravely ill, and crewmen carried her to the crowded Market Street Infirmary. She died shortly thereafter. Without any hesitation, the physicians attributed her death to yellow fever. Denial was at an end, and some physicians began to speak out publicly. With a sufficient body count accumulated in its wake, the "Stranger's Disease" was granted its proper name of yellow fever.[89]

Within days of the *Ruby* calamity, the editors of the *Times* demanded that the city clear up the decomposing cattle. Some citizens dragged many of the submerged animal carcasses onto the riverbank and skinned them for their hides. The result was a morbid display of carcasses lining the river and rotting under the summer sun.[90] The stench was such that no one could go "within a gunshot of the spot without smelling something stronger than cologne or the balm of a thousand flowers" to fortify one's abilities to withstand the odor. "A good deal of sickness will be the result if the nuisance is not abated at once."[91] *Ruby* was soon considered a plausible origin of the pestilence, if not at least a malodorous "feeder" exacerbating it.

A contrasting scene of comfort was found but blocks away. Holy Trinity Church was in its seventeenth year and growing. By the time of the *Ruby*'s demise, the parish had celebrated thus far that year twenty-seven baptisms, compared with only one funeral. The last funeral took place on March 14,

Patrick Gaughn — On the thirtieth of August, eighteen hundred and seventy three, I have buried Patrick Gaughn born in Ireland, who died on the same day, at Shreveport, at about the thirtieth year of his age. J. Pierre

Robert Gilfillin — On the sixth of November, eighteen hundred and seventy-three, I have buried Robert Gilfillin, born in Scotland who died on the previous day at Shreveport, at the age of fifty-three. J. J. Duffo, SJ

Entry from the funeral registry at Holy Trinity Church, recorded by Father Jean Pierre on August 30, 1873. The next entry is not until after the epidemic's end, recorded by Father James Duffo, SJ. *Courtesy of Holy Trinity Church, Shreveport, Louisiana.*

the day following Father Quémerais' baptism of the infant Francis. Father Pierre buried one of his parishioners, the twenty-seven-year-old French-born Clément Défèse.[92]

As the month of August reached its end, so, too, did the life of another parishioner. The August 30 Requiem Mass for Irishman Patrick Gaughn was just the second burial of the year and the last funeral Father Pierre ever recorded.[93] It was likely a funeral for a fever victim but held before such declarations. The sacristan and altar boys replaced all the gold candlesticks and their bleached candles with the silver sticks and darker candles. They changed the green Tabernacle veil to the violet one, removed all flowers from the high altar and put the Requiem altar cards into place and the black *Missale Defunctorum*, streaming with ribbons at length. No catafalque was required with the body present. The black pall with the embroidered silver cross was ready to completely drape the coffin to the floor when it arrived.

The black cope and processional cross were set in their proper places, with the holy water and aspergillum at the ready, so that the thirty-year-old Irishman might receive the proper farewell. A thurible was prepared with lit charcoal and incense bringing the sweet comfort of the Old World to the New World hinterlands, and the *Rituale Romanum*[94] was with a ribbon at the page for the Absolution over the body.

The *schola* knew the Gregorian chants, the ones Father Pierre preferred and identical to those sung in Brittany: the *Requiem aeternam* (Eternal Rest) and the longer Sequence *Dies irae* (Day of Wrath) and the final *Lux aeterna* (May Light Eternal). The Mass would last but thirty minutes, about the same time required to walk six blocks in solemn procession to the cemetery. Funeral processions from the church to the City Cemetery were mostly downhill and just over a half mile away but could be quite hot in summer. The altar boys, like the priest, wore their cassocks and surplices. Father placed the black stole around his neck. One server carried the processional cross and walked behind the thurifer with the incense bellowing.

Father Pierre followed the cross and led the body to its place of rest. For all the sadness of this recorded occasion, the sight would have been stirring, as among the last of the proper funerals for some time to come.

Implore God to Have Pity

The undersigned appeals to all those who believe in the efficacy of prayer, and beseeches them to implore God to have pity on us, and if it is His holy will to deliver us from sickness.
—Jean Pierre, priest, martyr to his charity

Office of Dr. Arie B. Snell, Corner of Market and Milam Streets, Shreveport
Monday, September 1, 1873
Commemoration of St. Giles, Abbot

The cool respite was over. The sun burned hot, allowing only a gentle breeze that merely "fanned the fevered brow." The second-floor office of Civil War veteran and physician Dr. Arie Snell was the site of an important assembly that balmy evening. Among those present were physicians, a few of the city ministers and prominent citizens. Following a protracted debate between the realists and the reluctant, together they formally, albeit begrudgingly, proclaimed the active presence of yellow fever within the community.[95]

The acknowledgement of yellow fever would be a debilitating economic blow. There would be pushback, as everyone in the room knew. Shreveport awakened the next day to the mitigated news of the presence of yellow fever, but not as an epidemic.

However, the corpses filling the mortuary spoke truth in no uncertain terms. There were, by that twentieth day of the outbreak, already twenty-nine recorded deaths.[96] Even so, the editors of the *Times*, whose pledged mission was to steadfastly serve as the "commercial and political paper devoted to the development of the material resources of Northwest Louisiana, Eastern Texas, and Southwest Arkansas," did not acknowledge the situation.[97] Weighing the evidence before them against the repercussions the news of the fever would bring, the physicians and newspaper editors thus condemned many who might otherwise have chosen to leave.

Meanwhile, people did begin to leave, by the hundreds. The day after the acknowledgement of yellow fever, the six-thirty morning train to Texas was more full than usual. The droves of people rushing the two o'clock afternoon train resembled nothing less than a stampede. Unabated for several days to come, each departing train overflowed as hundreds more anxious residents lined the tracks awaiting passage. Those who did not ride the rails hitched up wagons or rode on horseback. Some packed their steamer trunks and took to the riverboats. In a matter of days, Shreveport looked "depopulated," with approximately one-third of the population having fled.[98]

Leopold Baer, who owned a general mercantile on Texas Street, was one of the first to leave for healthier climes in early September. He was unknowingly infected with the virus when he arrived in Marshall, Texas, less than forty miles to the west, where he suffered and then died on September 8.[99] Many others who left were unaware they were similarly infected.

The rector of St. Mark's Episcopal Church and medical physician, Reverend Dr. William Tucker Dickinson Dalzell, himself a survivor of yellow fever years before, recognized the magnitude of the crisis. He skirted the notion of a minor fever problem and instead posted in the September 2 newspaper a request for "the men of Shreveport…to meet in the hall of the Board of Trade…to organize an association for the care and relief of the sick and needy."[100] The meeting was to be held that very morning.

When in his twenties, the Oxford-educated Dalzell helped organize relief during a cholera epidemic in Venezuela and later performed the same service during a yellow fever outbreak at Savannah, Georgia. Known among the South's leading authorities on epidemics, he had credibility. Dalzell had seen yellow fever before, and he recognized it in the faces of the sick and dying.[101]

On the centuries-old Feast of St. Giles on September 1, as he celebrated Mass, Father Pierre could only be mentally transported to his homeland and beloved church with its sights and smells, at the ancient chapel at Lanloup. There stood the statue of St. Loup[102] above the church's entrance, known to him in his childhood when he served as an altar boy. The parish priest would have them memorize the prayers *Ad Deum qui laetificat juventutem meam*... and their *Suscipiat Dominus* and all the postures and gestures, as altar boys had done for centuries. This he taught to young altar servers of his adopted home of Shreveport.

Father Pierre would have remembered the saints depicted there in glass and statuary. While looking at the likenesses of St. Giles and St. Blaise, among the Fourteen Holy Helpers, he learned to pray to them for protection against plagues. St. Blaise was the special patron of diseases of the throat, and Father Pierre held the memory of having newly blessed candles placed at his own throat every February.[103]

He knew their stories: Bishop Blaise, in Sebaste, Armenia,[104] in the year 316, imprisoned for refusing to renounce his faith, miraculously saved a young boy from choking on a fishbone, although that alone did not convince the governor to be merciful. Guards beat the saintly bishop and then ripped his flesh with iron combs before ultimately beheading him.

The statue of St. Giles, the only of the fourteen not killed for his faith, had a prime location on the high altar. At every Mass, Jean Pierre would have gazed upon him. "Sant Gilles" was one of the most popular saints of France and Germany. This seventh-century Athenian performed miracles but longed for a life of solitude and chose to live in a cave in France. Tradition holds that a God-sent deer nourished him with her milk. A hunter's arrow meant for the deer hit the saintly hermit, to the remorse of the hunter, who turned out to be the local king. St. Giles refused the king's physician and compensation but instead asked the king to build a monastery. He agreed, on the condition that Giles serve as its abbot. The arrow wound made St. Giles the patron of those with disabilities, specifically invoked for protection against plague.[105] St. Giles died peacefully around 720, not a martyr but, as the word *martyr* means, a true witness to the faith.[106]

It was these traditions that shaped the faith of Father Jean Pierre. His desire to study the faith appeared at the age of fourteen, and he entered the School of the Holy Virgin in Tréguier, having "satisfied the period of probationary approval."[107] He advanced to the minor seminary in Tréguier in 1849 at age eighteen and in 1852 entered the Grand Seminary of St. Brieuc. From there, he answered Bishop Martin's call to the frontier, where he found himself in 1873.[108]

The fifteenth-century church in Lanloup, France, hometown of Father Jean Pierre. *Authors' collection.*

Left: A statue of St. Blaise above the altar of the parish church in Lanloup, France, hometown of Father Jean Pierre. *Authors' collection.*

Below: The Grand Seminary at St. Brieuc, France, where Jean Pierre, Jean-Marie Biler and Francois Le Vézouët studied. *Authors' collection.*

Father Pierre continued the *Os iusti* Mass, the Mass for a sainted monk, for protection from diseases, that the people be spared the devastation experienced in fourteenth-century Europe. He proclaimed aloud the Gospel passage from St. Matthew:

> *Then Peter said to Jesus in reply, "We have given up everything and followed you. What will there be for us?" Jesus said to them, "...everyone who has given up houses or brothers or sisters or father or mother or children or lands for the sake of my name will receive a hundred times more, and will inherit eternal life."*[109]

After Mass, Father Pierre went to his office and met with John Caldwell and Julia Dufresne (née Lattier) to join them "in holy and lawful wedlock."[110] This eleventh wedding of the year took place in his office, as only one was Catholic and she had been married before. With proper dispensation, the brief but joyous ceremony concluded, with three of their friends serving as witnesses.

Father Pierre was a prime candidate for the episcopate, whose "excellent reputation had reached past the limits of [the] humble diocese" of Natchitoches. His mission work and steadfast faith attracted the attention of the hierarchy. In fact, many in the Church were seeking Father Pierre's removal from the minor diocese on the periphery to some more influential corner of the Catholic universe.[111] Bishop Martin's repeated insistence that Father Pierre remain in Shreveport was fortuitous.

In 1856, Father Pierre's fundraising, centered on tutoring children of wealthy non-Catholics, yielded monies for the construction of the first Catholic church, Holy Trinity, at Marshall and Fannin Streets. By 1873, after nearly twenty years of ministry, he had founded numerous remote missions and Catholic schools and established Shreveport's first public library in 1868, complete with subscription services.[112]

Father Pierre also mentored an orphan boy in residence at St. Mary's school. J.P. Schnell was fifteen when yellow fever was declared. They posed for a photograph together, with the priest pointing his finger to heaven and the teenager gazing upward, as if an apprentice, a future priest.[113]

The Catholic school in Shreveport dated to November 30, 1860, when Sister Theresa of Jesus and two other Daughters of the Cross came from Presentation Convent in Avoyelles Parish to establish St. Mary's Convent. Father Pierre shared a vision of Catholic education with Mother Mary Hyacinth, and he purchased property near Holy Trinity for that purpose.

Father Jean Pierre with an orphan boy in Shreveport, date unknown. *Courtesy of the Diocese of Alexandria, Louisiana.*

The enrollment response the first year required the construction of a second building in 1861. The outbreak of the Civil War meant a decline in enrollment, but this was the core of what later became St. Vincent's Academy for girls in Fairfield. The students there were almost entirely Protestant and Jewish.[114] Now, the forty-five-year-old priest was about to confront the greatest challenge of his ministry.

At ten o'clock the next morning, a few citizens met at the Board of Trade for the called public meeting. They gathered "around the green baize covered table, over which trade and railroads and stocks were [once] discussed."[115] The meeting was in the same room where festivities surrounding the opening of the Texas and Pacific Railroad were planned.[116] The topic now was the need to organize a charitable response for the ill. Among those around the table was Father Jean Pierre.

Absent from that first meeting was Father Quémerais, who was one week from his twenty-sixth birthday and frequently ill. Recovering at the O'Neill home in Bossier Parish, he immediately responded to Father Pierre's call to return, even as "consumption was consuming him" and he "was not thought to live long."[117]

An enhanced photograph of Father Isidore Quémerais from a larger family photograph. *Image provided by Pierre Mouazé, a family descendant.*

Baptized with the name Isidore, the patron saint of farmers, Father Quémerais hailed from the rural village of Pleine-Fougères in the Archdiocese of Rennes. His sharp mind, piety and devotion compensated for what he lacked in physical stamina. Contributing to his missionary calling was quick mastery of the English language. Father Quémerais, with rare selfless charisma, and described as a Franco-southern gentleman,[118] proved invaluable to Father Pierre.

The primary question at the Board of Trade was how to best care for the "sick-poor," working poor families, freedmen and immigrants. There was no shortage of street urchins, ragmen and tramps with no means to escape the city, all facing an equalizing fate at the hand of yellow fever.[119] The charity hospital was still more of an idea than an institution. The U.S. Marine Hospital was not suitable, especially with no guaranteed support from the federal government. Instead, residents organized a private association, reliant on donations, and utilized all the political, social, religious and commercial connections their leaders could muster.

Those community leaders formed the local chapter of the Howard Association, named for the British social justice pioneer John Howard (1726–1790). Many Howard Association chapters formed in America in the mid-nineteenth century in response to yellow fever. They fundraised, organized caregivers and coordinated relief efforts across the American South.[120] The Shreveport chapter began with nineteen founding members. Within the first of its resolutions was found the following plea: "Anyone who is familiar with the treatment of yellow fever desiring to offer their services as nurses will please give their names."[121]

Besides medical relief, Father Pierre and Father Quémerais sought also to sanctify plague-ridden Shreveport by continuing the sacraments for Roman Catholics. They offered Mass daily and prayed with the afflicted, regardless of creed, class or race. They anointed sick Catholics and witnessed no

Photograph of the Quémerais family, with Father Isidore Quémerais at center back. *Image provided by Pierre Mouazé, a family descendant.*

shortage of burials. What no one foresaw was the digging of a trench on the southwest corner of the City Cemetery[122] as a single mass grave. There was no other time in Shreveport history when the need for compassionate Christian care was so crucial as when death loomed so near to so many.

Yet steamers continued to come and go from Shreveport, indifferent to the growing concern. The steamer *Texas* left for New Orleans the same day the Shreveport Howard Association formed. Throughout the first week of September, business continued as usual, without regard to the declaration of the presence of yellow fever.[123]

In fact, the *Daily Shreveport Times* reported skepticism in the face of mounting evidence to the contrary: "From what we learn there is no doubt but the reports of the prevailing sickness in this city are greatly exaggerated abroad."[124] Within its pages, such denials were typeset inches from reports that the paper's own senior editor, foreman of the office and three printers were all down with the fever, while another staffer was absent because his entire family was stricken.[125]

Polarizing outlooks set in. By the September 3 edition, a local druggist was posting daily temperatures monitoring spread of disease, city merchants were advertising products dedicated to "convalescing" and the Howard Association published its first mortuary report of yellow fever victims. Three recorded deaths in the city on September 3 were attributed to the disease. The city's Board of Administrators appropriated $500 to purchase medicine and ice and to hire nurses. Relentless in denial, on this day the newspaper reported, "The fury of the disease seems to have expended itself on its victims and to be now dying out. There has been much greater scare than there was cause for....Our advice is to keep cool mentally and physically."[126]

Many theorized the illness was related to poorly serviced outhouses and open pits of sewage.[127] Proponents of this theory were approaching the cause but did not know exactly how these conditions related. No one fathomed the critical link between the life cycle of the mosquito and conditions for the species to thrive—or that they could transmit a virus. That connection was not made for three more decades.

City officials ordered men to spread lime throughout gutters and standing water. The same men placed tar barrels in the streets and burned them to release dense clouds of black smoke,[128] a practice thought to rid the atmosphere of poisonous vapors or "miasma." The fumes indeed helped, somewhat, but by unintentionally repelling mosquitos. At Holy Trinity, there was comforting contrast in the fragrant smoke of incense, along with prayers Father Pierre and Father Quémerais offered for those buried without a Requiem Mass. Both priests offered the Mass of the Dead and prayed the *De profundis* from the altars in the church where fewer and fewer people were present.

With the thermometer reaching eighty-seven degrees on Wednesday, September 3, the plumes of tar turned the city into a reeking furnace. On this day, the Howard Association assigned Father Pierre to work Fever Ward 1 of Shreveport, along with eight other men. They ranged in age from store clerk Otto Schnurr, seventeen, to J.W. Booth, fifty-three, a painter from England. Two were in the medical field: Dr. W.S. Donaldson, age unknown, and R. Hyams, thirty-six, a druggist from South Carolina. L.R. Simmons, thirty years old, a future newspaper editor, served as Howard Association president. Others were R.H. Lindsay, thirty-nine, a cotton factor and

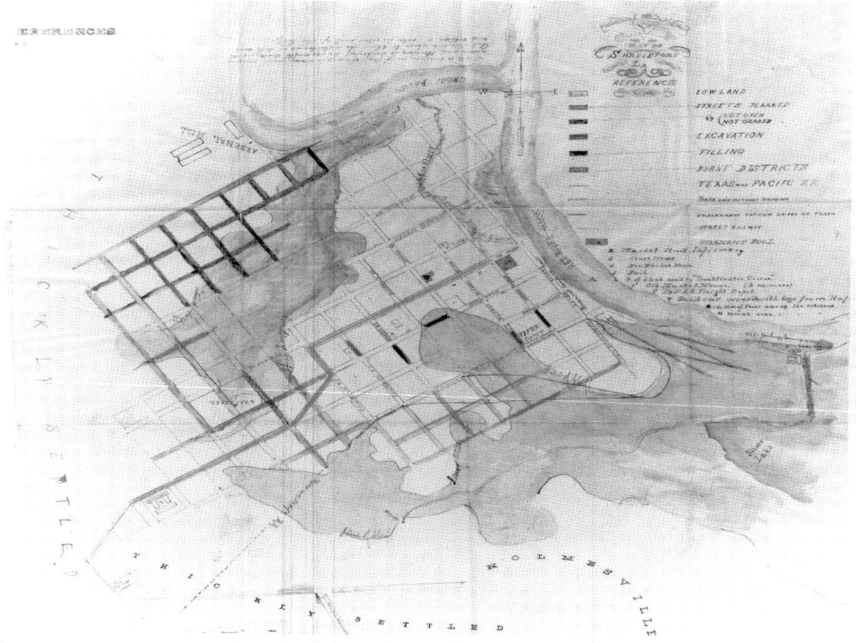

Map drawn by University of Kentucky medical student Augustine Booth, showing areas of infection in Shreveport in 1873. *Courtesy of Noel Archives and Special Collections, Louisiana State University at Shreveport.*

immigrant from Scotland; Tom Bylan, forty, ship's carpenter from Ohio; and J.J. Horan, thirty-seven, saddle maker from Ireland.[129]

The nine volunteers, including Father Pierre, covered twenty-eight blocks, between Common Street and the river, bounded on the other two ends by the north side of Texas Street and Caddo Street. Dr. Donaldson had experience with yellow fever from his tenure in Norfolk, Virginia, during the outbreak of 1855.[130] This ward's allotment of compassionate and capable men probably made this team among the best.

The Howards made no distinction among patients based on class or economic status. Yellow fever spread so rapidly, and the demand for aid was so pervasive, that "there were none so proud that they did not claim assistance; there were none so poor and outcast that its succor did not reach them."[131] In their first week, they nursed, fed and provided basic comfort. When the fever was triumphant, they shifted to the macabre task of digging graves. The poorest were brought to a temporary hospital, established at the opulent opera house, Talley's, on Milam Street in Fever

Ward 2.[132] Cruel necessity transformed a playground of the rich into the sick house of the poor.

That evening, the steamer *Royal George* arrived with cotton bales from Jefferson, Texas. Two other steamers left Shreveport for New Orleans. While other Gulf of Mexico ports imposed a quarantine against the Crescent City, New Orleans was still allowing traffic from just about anywhere. Shreveport was destined to have its contact with the outside world—including the revered river traffic—for but a precious while longer.[133]

Also departing Shreveport that day was the Texas and Pacific Railroad train to Dallas. At the Dallas city limits, the engineer braked as he saw a fire on the freshly laid railroad track. Armed men boarded the train, threatening to shoot anyone who attempted to leave—claiming they would even kill the engineer if he attempted to move the train in either direction. This was no train robbery. It was enforcement of mandatory quarantine, but in the unique Texas way. Cooler heads prevailed, and the train was allowed to depart for Shreveport the next morning but made no progress toward Dallas.[134]

The noose of the quarantine tightened. As panic spread throughout Texas, on Friday morning, September 5, the mayor of Jefferson declared, "This dire disease is raging in Shreveport and would play havoc with us in every way."[135] Shreveport editors responded with several inches of a lead column lambasting the "vicious…rattle brained" editors of Jefferson's paper. The two cities were partners in times of economic prosperity, and mutual interests were directly at stake.[136]

The ongoing denial of the Shreveport paper, attributing deaths to "excessive drinking," heart disease and even "swamp fever," rather than yellow fever, contrasted obvious reality. Meanwhile, single-minded in their compassionate ministry, Father Pierre and Father Quémerais labored night and day. They saw a little hope, as there had been fewer than ten interments of victims in the past two days.[137] Father Pierre, in the midst of his selfless service, made this request in the newspaper:

> *The undersigned appeals to all those who believe in the efficacy of prayer, and beseeches them to implore God to have pity on us, and if it is His holy will to deliver us from sickness.*
> *Respectfully,*
> *Father J. Pierre*

Undoubtedly, Father Pierre remembered 1858. After the construction of Holy Trinity Church and during a month-long tenure in Bayou Pierre, he fell ill with a debilitating unnamed fever. He penned a desperate note to Bishop Martin: "I have been sick here for six days, nailed to the bed, still burning with intense fever.…If this does not leave me, I ardently desire you send a priest from Natchitoches to give me the last Sacraments."[138]

As six more were buried in the City Cemetery, including the circus ringmaster, Dallas and Longview, Texas, established more official, if less martial, quarantines.[139] A Texas newspaper correspondent wrote: "There is one awful characteristic about the sickness, and that is, that no one has recovered. Some are what they say doing well. One day you hear of a case doing well.…The next day a corpse is awaiting the hearse."[140]

The entire nation followed the crisis in Shreveport. Major newspapers began following the story. By mid-October, even the *New York Times* reported, "Hundreds have fallen victim to the terrible scourge," and "The fever there [in Shreveport] is of such a malignant type.…All who are seized with it drop off like sheep dying with the rot."[141]

Only outdoor Masses could be celebrated since public health officials decreed no groups could gather indoors. Sunday and daily Masses continued, yellow fever or not. Father Pierre and Father Quémerais wore green and prayed the Mass of the Fourteenth Sunday after Pentecost. The faithful beseeched God's mercy, as their pastor had asked, and sought the protection of the Fourteen Holy Helpers. On this day, Matthew 6:24–33 sealed a common theme: "Do not worry about your life, what you will eat or drink, or about your body.…Can any of you by worrying add a single moment to your life-span?…Seek first the kingdom of God."[142]

These were comforting words, like the words the people had heard often the past week, as both priests offered the Votive Mass *in tempore mortalitatis* for the Deliverance in Time of Pestilence:

> *Please, Lord, as You commanded the fever of Simon Peter's mother-in-law to depart, command an end to this plague besetting our people! People brought you their sick and with but a touch from You, You healed them. Look upon the faithful who seek Your healing touch. You expelled demons. Rebuke them!*
> *In Thy clemency withdraw the scourge of Thy wrath.*[143]

Just a few blocks away from Holy Trinity, representatives of the Howards went to the Western Union telegraph office. Through the wires, they advised their chapters in St. Louis and New Orleans that the fever situation in Shreveport was now "epidemic and on the increase," and immediate aid was needed in the form of nurses, physician volunteers and relief supplies.[144]

Except for rail, Shreveport was now completely isolated by land routes. One Shreveporter posted a letter delivered by train to "Jack" in Jefferson, Texas: "The yellow fever has come, and like some awful black pall, thrown its pestilential folds about us, spreading fright, terror and death among us." Yet river traffic remained officially open, and familiar riverboats continued to arrive.[145]

The time was coming when Shreveport would stand alone.

Blotted Out of Existence

Whole families were swept away, and commercial firms, partners and clerks, were literally blotted out of existence.
—Daily Shreveport Times, *November 15, 1873*

Shreveport, Fever Ward 2
Tuesday, September 9, 1873
The Commemoration of St. Gorgonius, martyr

The suffering within Talley's Opera House, now a makeshift hospital, was exacerbated by the heat. The summer was burning itself out in an intensity that marked the last days of the humid season. In the evening hours, a cool and gusty breeze often prevailed. Rumor held that the vying atmospheric conditions provided the "bread and meat" for the disease to flourish. Shreveport druggists now agreed to remain open twenty-four hours a day.[146]

Father Isidore Quémerais, with no time to celebrate his twenty-sixth birthday as he had each ninth day of September, prayed the Office and then a private Mass at the side altar of Holy Trinity. People no longer called on the priests, even for important matters. Neither priest made new entries in the sacramental registers, as there were no baptisms, weddings or funeral Masses.[147] Meanwhile, the *Daily Shreveport Times* relented and confirmed a yellow fever outbreak. The epidemic was almost a month old, and finally, public denials ceased.[148]

Father Quémerais went to the bedsides of wealthy and poor, anointed the Catholics and whispered comfort to all. The now twenty-six-year-old curate spent himself into exhaustion and sacrificed his own precarious health. There were many new fever cases that day and twelve more burials.[149] This meant twelve more emaciated bodies mixed with the upland Louisiana clay and hastily tossed lime. Twelve more souls released to judgment.[150]

An ominous bonfire lit the riverbank south of the stricken city that evening. With no action by public officials or the commercial interests for the wrecked steamer *Ruby*, a rogue citizen broke through the quarantine to set fire to the wreck. Melting animal fat added to the conflagration and extinguished only as the flames reached the waterline. *Ruby*, still considered the breeding ground of the pestilence, was a nuisance no more.[151] As the *Ruby* smoldered in the river, Father Pierre readied an urgent dispatch to Marshall:

> *Send us all the Sisters of Charity you can spare to our city, as soon as possible. All arrangements will be made to take care of them.*
> *Father J. Pierre*[152]

The sisters based in Marshall, Texas, were ready. Nearer, of course, were the Daughters of the Cross at the convent of St. Vincent's in Fairfield. With the start of classes postponed, Father Pierre knew the Daughters of the Cross would help. While still in their native France in 1855, Father Pierre approached Mother Hyacinth about the possibility of educating his niece. He also mentioned that he would soon join Bishop Auguste Martin to begin missionary work in Louisiana.[153] Mother Mary Hyacinth was instantly intrigued. Eventually, the bishop approved her and nine other daughters to institute Louisiana missions. Throughout the 1850s and 1860s, the sisters established chapter houses in New Orleans and Alexandria, Louisiana.

Fever infected the Fairfield convent several days before Father Pierre's dispatch reached them. Most of the sisters were too ill to help.[154] In Marshall, the Sisters of Charity answered Father Pierre's call and boarded the Texas and Pacific Railroad. The railroad ignored the quarantine and let the sisters pass to render aid. With volunteers greatly diminished, Shreveport desperately needed the help.

The New Orleans Howard Association sent a dispatch on September 10 requesting an update on Shreveport. They received the anticipated response that the city needed nurses and physicians, although there was little hope to pay them. The New Orleans Howards promised to send three physicians and eight nurses the following morning, pledging that the people of New

Orleans would cover their expenses.[155] Father Pierre, although feeling an understandable fatigue, was relieved to hear a second wave of assistance was coming.[156] Certainly, he thought a little food and a few hours' sleep would renew his stamina.

†

On the river, a sense of duty also gripped Lieutenant Eugene Woodruff. He joined the fight against the disease in Fever Ward 2, leaving his brother George and crew behind on the snagboat *Aid*. Woodruff volunteered with the Howards and began organizing the hospital in Talley's Opera House, overlapping efforts with Father Quémerais.[157] In a letter he wrote to his mother on September 9, he shrugged off the danger, reassuring her:

> *We are all in excellent health....I do not consider myself in any danger for two reasons. First my life insurance policy is made to cover the risk by a permit received in June from the home company. Second, my system is in good condition to resist attacks, and I am not in the least afraid....For myself you need not worry.*[158]

So resolute was Woodruff to remain in Shreveport that he refused an army order to leave until the epidemic passed.[159]

South of Shreveport and miles inland from the river, Father Jean Marie Biler was also on the front line fighting despair. A messenger raced to the Fairfield convent on Tuesday, September 9, with a new appeal from Father Pierre to the mother superior asking her to send as many sisters as she could spare.[160] The messenger handed a second letter to Father Biler, begging his help.[161] Immediately after Mass, he headed to the fever wards to join Father Quémerais and Father Pierre.[162] With no thought to his life, he, too, turned his energy toward death-ridden Shreveport.

Reinforcing their efforts were Sister Mary of the Cross and Sister Mary Angela, who had been at St. Mary's since early September. At Father Pierre's request, the mother superior sent others: Sister Mary Seraphina, Sister Mary Vincent and Sister Mary Martha.[163] Sister Mary Martha soon ministered with Father Pierre. Also a native of France, Sister Mary Martha was born in 1828 and baptized as Marie Françoise Déné. She was an original member of the Daughters of the Cross who came to America in 1855.[164]

Shreveport was increasingly isolated, as the *Times* reported: "Owing to the want of compositors, we are unable to issue more than a half sheet for the present. We will do better as soon as the epidemic will permit. As it is, we are doing well to get even that out." The newspaper's staff dwindled to just one adult male and two boys to work the press, craft the stories and set the type. Ironically, this swift effect spoke to the epidemic the editors had adamantly denied a week before.[165]

Father Jean Marie Biler. *Image from prayer card.*

By the second week of September, interments were so frequent that the dead received little ceremony. Volunteers had buried approximately 120 residents since September began, a figure that did not include deceased refugees.[166] With exhaustion setting in among dwindling volunteers, the dying required more care than the living could offer. The 3 priests took turns commending souls to the Lord and then blessing and sprinkling with holy water the bodies in the mass grave at the City Cemetery. The *New York Times* reprinted this from a Shreveport resident:

> *We no longer* [have] *funerals; the hearses, followed by one or two carriages, dashed through the streets like sections of artillery in a battle seeking a position; enough men* [are] *drummed up, often with difficulty, to lift the coffin into the hearse and the body* [is] *borne away to the cemetery as swiftly as decency…permit*[s].[167]

On September 12, the sky drew up in a curtain of gray cloud cover that unleashed a "fine thunder shower accompanied by a copious rain."[168] From his home in Fever Ward 4 off Fairfield Avenue, between St. Vincent's and the commercialized town, Caddo Parish judge Henry Gerard Hall—with little work to be done as no trials were scheduled—used his free time to write in his diary: "A bountiful rain came a little after noon, a great blessing to us in many respects, filling our cistern, reviving our potatos [*sic*], peas & other vegetation & giving us hope of turnips. I hope also the rain may help to arrest the sickness which so fearfully prevails."[169]

The "great blessing" of a "bountiful rain" that swelled the judge's cistern brought other effects. The rains produced stagnant pools and widened the muddy lowlands, soon teeming with mosquito larvae, and also extinguished the burning tar barrels. The life cycle of the mosquito *Aedes aegypti* meant that the many eggs laid following the rain would form adult mosquitoes within a few days. The judge's own cistern became a prime breeding ground for the mosquito.

As entire families and commercial enterprises were being "blotted out of existence" by yellow fever,[170] the newspaper began reporting on conditions of surrounding towns, faring little better than Shreveport. Nearby locales reported yellow fever deaths, some of whom were infected before fleeing Shreveport. As outbreak reports came from as far away as Galveston and Houston, Texas, more of the eastern Texas towns instituted quarantines. The Louisiana press mocked the reactions of their western neighbors; a contemporary joke was that Texas was experiencing an unfortunate "quarantine epidemic."[171]

Shreveport's commercial lifeblood of riverboat traffic only gradually slowed, in stark contrast to the strict and immediate quarantine by rail, stage, horse and foot. On Saturday, September 13, the steamer *13th Era* departed Shreveport with two hundred head of cattle and several passengers for New Orleans—freely moving from one quarantined city to another. Meanwhile, other steamers,[172] hindered only by low waters, were expected any day. Yet, as the *13th Era* departed the dock across from Levee Street, its officers reported that they gladly left "for some more healthy locality."[173]

This was among the last commercial activity, as steamboat agents sent word to New Orleans that there would be no freight to send back and mused there could soon be no one left to pay for future deliveries anyway.[174] The United States Post Office stagecoaches came only intermittently and even then refused to enter town, stopping outside the quarantine and exchanging mail sacks across the river or other body of water—assumed to be a safe boundary.[175] The grip of death was wrenching the life of Shreveport's citizens but also its livelihood; even knowledge of the rest of the world was slipping away.

Public groaning over the nuisance of the now-defunct circus was growing. With the *Ruby* and its grisly cargo gone, people searched for other reasons for the sickness. Suspicion fell to the peculiar "carnies" who remained encamped with their tents, wagonloads of curiosities and livestock at Milam and Edwards Streets in Fever Ward 2, close to the Howards' hospital for the poor.

Many of the circus entertainers contracted the fever; some showed a resilience and recovered, attributed to the transient nature of circus life or potential previous exposure. Soon enough, residents called for the removal of the circus and for the seizure of their "trunks, clothes, and other articles capable of holding infectious poison," with the intention that all "should be burned up, no matter what their value."[176]

Circus official John Dingess said of the closing in Shreveport:

> *After the tour of the state of Texas, and toward the end of the travelling season, the establishment arrived at Shreveport, Louisiana, where the performances of the company came to an abrupt termination by the appearance of Yellow Fever in its worst form. Everyone appeared panic-stricken and began to hasten away with all possible speed; many however, who were unable to get away, fell victims to the dreaded disease. All the performers and musicians, together with the writer and several other attaches, embarked at midnight on a steam packet bound for St. Louis, Missouri, which was the last steamer to leave that port for many weeks.*[177]

The rest of the country remained eager for news about Shreveport. Three New Orleans volunteer physicians[178] sent a dispatch laden with stark clarity to the world, which was reprinted in the *New York Times*: "No report you may have received from here can possibly exaggerate the condition of affairs. They are indeed deplorable."[179]

"Good Father Biler," as the mother superior called him, returned to the convent Saturday evening for a retreat with the sisters, who prepared to solemnly renew their Holy Vows.[180] Their joy to see him quickly turned to concern, for he "brought the sad news that Father Pierre was unwell and Father Quémerais completely exhausted from fatigue."[181] The convent's chaplain ate a light supper and then returned to town, promising he would be back at the convent the next morning for Sunday Mass.[182]

One Great Charnel House

Shreveport is one great hospital—one great charnel house, and the Times, *merely a death record.*
—Daily Shreveport Times, *September 17, 1873*

St. Mary Catholic School, Fever Ward I
Sunday, September 14, 1873
Fifteenth Sunday after Pentecost, Exaltation of the Holy Cross

Father Quémerais could not rise from bed, so great was his fatigue. He was a priest without a Mass, and it was a Sunday without a homily. Father Pierre, also fatigued, was determined to celebrate the Sunday Mass for his people, who had begun to express a benign acceptance of the constant presence of death.

That week, the occasional afternoon shower cleaned the atmosphere and fell on those yet living. The same rain shifted the dead lying in the mass grave. A doctor advised that the healthy population should exercise little and limit exposure to other people, as well as the outdoor elements.[183] With the exception of the Howards, the sisters, processions and city police, the people of Shreveport were living and dying in solitude, in corner rooms and on upper floors above family storefronts—a tragic honeycomb of quarantines within the quarantine.

Father Pierre was anxious about his assistant and found it impossible to rest on Sunday, although already clearly ill himself. In the previous week, he and Sister Mary Martha had walked within the quarantine bravely and tirelessly. The two stepped onto porches and knocked on doors and, when opened, entered to go to bedsides of those in need. The sights and smells that awaited them became as familiar as birdsong. They abandoned concern for their own safety as they wiped foreheads and held hands of the dying, praying with them. They knew they were in the presence of the disease and yet feared not for themselves. They were heeding Christ's command, in Matthew 25, to visit the sick, believing that as often as they cared for them, they were caring for Jesus Himself.

In one such visit, a frantic father thrust his baby girl into Sister Mary Martha's arms. As Father Pierre prayed at the bedside of the sick mother, the newborn died in the sister's arms.[184] This emotional visit made such an impression that they took time from the day's work to write about it before proceeding to the next house. The pace of the work exacted a toll on them both.

The plight of Shreveport continued to be a national sensation, helped by the exertions of newspapermen and telegraph operators. Operator George J. Rae, in a dying delirium in Fever Ward 2, would never again hear the familiar click-click-click of the telegraph key. From the *New York Times* to the *Helena (Montana) Weekly Herald*, national newspapers provided frequent updates on the growing crisis. By mid-September, it was estimated that more than 10 percent of the remaining population was badly ill—not counting those already dead.[185] The commerce-minded founding fathers of Shreveport had hoped to get the fledgling city on the United States map, but not like this.

In a residence not far from the riverfront, a new bride lay ill only days after her wedding. She wrote this testimony:

> *Graves were filled as fast as they could be dug. All during the night horses could be heard carrying the dead, and the moans and weeping of the bereaved families swept over the town. Girls who were well today were dead from the terrible fever in a week's time. My husband was in the upper story of the house where we were living at the time and I was downstairs. There were days when I watched for them to carry up a casket for him, or maybe bring one to me. We were so sick, the plans had been made for our burial together.*[186]

The editors of the *Times*, also in Saturday's edition, proclaimed in utter exhaustion of the subject, "We hardly know what to say regarding the increase or decrease of the fever, opinions vary so much."[187]

It was an easier task to simply count the bodies. The daily mortuary report furnished by the Howard Association became the measuring stick of the epidemic's strength. Were there more dead than yesterday? Yes? The fever is on the rise. No? The fever is drawing to a close. The result was a constant cycle of hope and despair. Meanwhile, both the wealthy and the poor were drawn to final rest, and their ends came in a ceaseless and ceremony-free procession. For the city's prominent, "death brought down the scepter to the level of the spade."[188]

Father Biler returned as promised in the early morning to offer Sunday Mass for the sisters, to lead them in the Ceremony of the Renewal of their Holy Vows and to expose, as was their custom, the Blessed Sacrament in the monstrance for adoration throughout the day.[189] Meanwhile, Father Quémerais, who had selflessly labored to the point of exhaustion,[190] agreed to cease only when a physician ordered bed rest, and within a few days, his diagnosis was officially yellow fever.[191] The small Catholic community clung to every update on his condition, which was indeed worrying to all—symbolic, even, of the fate of the young town on the verge of collapse. Available medicines may have helped relieve his pain, but Father Quémerais offered his suffering, as he told so many others to do, for the good of the souls in purgatory.

The actual fever phase normally lasted about seventy-two hours. Some infected were overwhelmed by the violent intensity of the attack, and those mercifully died quickly—perhaps by the end of the second day. The young father lingered far longer. Following a sudden end of fever, his dying body transitioned into the "calm stage," with convulsions ceasing and his pulse dropping below an average rate.[192] Caregivers gave him ice to chew on as he was able to comply.[193] What happened next, according to the doctors, determined whether he would live or die. If Father Quémerais's body had defeated the virus, he would begin to show signs of increasing cognition and a desire to move about.

The arithmetic of the mortality grew beyond shocking and approached a logistical quandary. On September 14, Judge Henry G. Hall noted in his journal that there were "twenty-one burials at 5:00 pm today, mostly strangers to me."[194] Indeed, between September 11 and 16, the mortality rate reached its peak. The ill were "dropped off like sheep dying with the rot" by family members entrusting them to unknown physicians. Only the pharmacies and makeshift hospitals remained open. The local paper punctuated the situation: "Shreveport is one great hospital, one great charnel house, and the *Times*, merely a death record."[195]

Father Jean Pierre. *Image from prayer card.*

One great charnel house. Shreveporters knew the archaic expression as a place where human remains are stored in the absence of either propriety or ceremony, sometimes inferring disrespect or lack of concern for the dead. The Shreveport charnel house reflected not a disrespect for the dead but, rather, an inability to properly care for them. Shreveport was reduced to such careless disposal of remains that every negative image of history was conjured. As the charnel-house priests of Shreveport worked *in persona Christi*, in the context of widespread human suffering, the eyes of the world took notice.

As his assistant's condition briefly stabilized, Father Pierre's worsened. The stalwart French priest the city had come to know and love "refused to go to bed when so many were pleading the consolation of the Church in their last hours."[196] Father Pierre would not allow the city to be without the sacraments.

The Fifteenth Sunday after Pentecost providentially fell on September 14. All the faithful contemplated, as the Church had on that date every year since the seventh century, the glory of the Cross, as the first words of the Mass directed them to do through the *Introit.* Although ill with fever, Father Pierre celebrated the Mass as if it were his first Mass, his only Mass, his last Mass. The faithful prayed the *Collect*: "May we who have known mystery [of the cross] on earth, also be worthy to enjoy in heaven the happiness which it has purchased for us."[197] As he read aloud the epistle, Father Pierre prayed that they all would be as obedient to death of yellow fever as Jesus was obedient unto death on a cross,[198] if the will of God.[199] Each prayer fortified those present: "May my service be pleasing to You, O Lord."[200] "O Lord our God, we are preparing to receive the Body and Blood of our Lord Jesus Christ....Grant that we may also enjoy for all eternity the salvation it has purchased for us."[201] As the Masses concluded in both Shreveport and Fairfield, they prayed: "Be close to us, O Lord our God."[202]

†

Following Mass at the convent, Father Biler quickly ate breakfast and hastened back to town, saying he would return in the evening for Benediction.[203] After Mass at Holy Trinity, Father Pierre was determined to ensure that every Catholic who needed the Last Rites received it, fatigued though he was. Father Quémerais' condition remained such that Father Pierre did not anoint him, as he was in that indeterminate calm state. Shortly thereafter, fever seized Father Pierre just as his assistant took a turn for the worse. The unimaginable happened: both priests were deathly ill. Word of Father Pierre's diagnosis did not reach Father Biler before he departed to return to the convent. He arrived at Fairfield at seven o'clock, bringing only the certain news that Father Quémerais had a very critical case of yellow fever.[204]

The true outlook for Father Pierre was grim. The public received the news the next day that he was "dangerously sick." The newspaper lauded his heroism and anticipated his death, calling it "deplored" by the people even before he passed on. Meanwhile, Father Biler continued working at a constant, maddening pace, the impossible work of three priests now left to only one.[205] In his turn, he also devoted every moment to comforting the sick and dying,[206] resting only when he collapsed.

As Father Jean Pierre lay on his deathbed, two weeks shy of turning fifty-two and a week away from his eighteenth anniversary of priesthood, another servant of the epidemic working with the second fever ward became noticeably ill: Lieutenant Eugene A. Woodruff.[207] Woodruff was living in town at the Elstner home at Spring and Fannin Streets. They had already survived a bout of yellow fever so had a perceived clinical immunity.

On Monday morning, September 15, Father Quémerais' temperature spiked again, the convulsions returned and he began to vomit blood, the most ominous of signs.[208] His caregivers gave him as much ice as he would take and caressed his hot and dry skin. The headache would remain to the end, agonizing in its intensity.[209]

Father Biler came to his bedside with holy water and the *Rituale Romanum* to anoint his fellow Breton and brother priest. Father Biler could not rouse Father Quémerais:

> Je suis ici. *I am here, your brother, Jean Marie. Isidore, I prepare you to meet your Redeemer. Kiss the holy crucifix.*
>
> Je suis ici, ton frère, Jean Marie. Isidore, je te prépare à rencontrer ton Rédempteur. Embrasse le saint crucifix.

With every move executed with reverence, he sprinkled holy water in the form of a cross on Father Quémerais and then the room and on those standing by, saying in Latin: "*Aspérges me, Dómine*…'Purify me with hyssop, Lord, and I shall be clean of sin. Wash me, and I shall be whiter than snow.' (Psalms 51)"

He lit a candle and said in the language of the Church: "Our help is in the name of the Lord." Everyone responded without hesitation: "Who made heaven and earth."

Father Biler continued the ritual: "Lord Jesus Christ, let your angels of peace take over and put down all wicked strife. May almighty God have mercy on you, forgive you your sins, and lead you to everlasting life. May the almighty and merciful Lord grant you pardon, absolution, and remission of your sins."

He dipped his thumb in the holy oil and traced the sign of the cross on Father Quémerais' eyelids, asking mercy for any evil done through the power of sight. Likewise, he anointed each ear, for sins committed through the power of hearing, and then his nose and mouth. He then took his hands and, for the first time in an act reserved for moribund priests, anointed the back of the hands, not the palms as he had done for so many of the laity of late, and then his feet. He prayed the litany:

> Kýrie eléison. Christe eléison. Kýrie eléison.
> *Holy Mary, pray for him.*
> *All holy angels and archangels, pray for him.*
> *Holy Abel,*
> *All choirs of the just,*
> *Holy Abraham,*
> *St. John the Baptist,*
> *St. Joseph,*
> *All holy patriarchs and prophets,*
> *St. Peter,*
> *St. Paul,*
> *St. Andrew,*
> *St. John,*
> *All holy apostles and evangelists,*
> *All holy disciples of our Lord,*
> *All holy Innocents,*
> *St. Stephen,*
> *St. Lawrence,*
> *All holy martyrs…*

> *By the authority granted me by the Holy See, I impart to you a plenary indulgence and the remission of all your sins; and I bless you in the name of the Father, and of the Son, and of the Holy Spirit. Amen.*

With the sign of the cross at the ritual's conclusion, Father Biler spoke words of consolation. "Isidore, resist the temptations of the devil, and if death comes, go peacefully in the Lord." Before he departed for Fairfield, Father Biler commended Father Quémerais' soul to God, as death was imminent. He informed the sisters that he had administered the final sacraments to Father Quémerais,[210] and only later did they learn that "the good young priest died at 7 o'clock the evening of the 15th."[211]

The other bad news Father Biler announced was that their dear Sister Mary Martha, the one into whose arms was thrust the dying infant just the week before, also had yellow fever. Father Biler had no appetite, but at Mother's insistence, he tried to take some supper before making funeral arrangements for Father Quémerais.[212]

The Busy Carnival of Misery

Yet we believe we may pause in the midst of the solemn scenes that surround us: that we may snatch a moment from the busy carnival of misery to express the deep regret of this community at the death of the Reverend Father Pierre. This pious priest, kindly and most excellent man, was seized of the fever Saturday evening and died Tuesday evening.

—Daily Shreveport Times, *September 18, 1873*

Road to Shreveport, below the Quarantine Line
Tuesday, September 16, 1873
Feast of Saints Cornelius, pope, and Cyprian, bishop, martyrs

Shreveport mayor Samuel Levy posted a proclamation in the September 15 newspaper, the same day the soul of Father Quémerais was commended to God. He announced an auxiliary branch of city government in the Talley building (not to be confused with the Talley's Opera House) to oversee estate settlements, death certificates and burial matters.[213] It was an efficient system for the practical settlement of final affairs.

Confidence in the fever's abatement was waning, with the newspaper reporting that "the number of deaths are fearful to contemplate. The mortality is beyond precedent and it looks as though comparatively few will get well. In some…instances whole families have been swept out of existence in the short space of one week."[214] Survivors gathered the possessions of the dead to burn, and sometimes even the dwellings were burned.[215] Instinctively, as in ages past, confused and desperate survivors burned the vestiges of all touched by death. As in those grim ages before, death did not respect the earthly element of fire.

With little sleep and already ill himself, Father Biler reentered the quarantine to bury Father Quémerais. He had a brief Requiem Mass, but unlike hundreds of yellow fever victims whose final resting place was a mass grave without ceremony, the young priest from Pleine-Fougères received a proper and dignified, albeit hasty, burial in the City Cemetery. Not far from the mass grave, he was placed in a private plot donated by grieving parishioners.[216]

Later that day when doctors despaired of saving "dear Father Pierre,"[217] Father Biler went to his bedside and, for the second day in a row, anointed the backs of two more hands and prayed the Litany of Saints. As Father Pierre was conscious, Father Biler offered him Holy Communion as *viaticum*, food for the journey. Father Biler stayed with him until the end. When Father Pierre expressed surprise that Father Quémerais did not visit him, it was Dr. Joseph Moore who informed him, "Father Quémerais has preceded you to Heaven; you will soon go to see him."[218]

Father Biler added the commendation prayers meant for a person literally at the moment of death, which he could not pray for Father Quémerais the day prior:

> *Depart, Christian soul, from this world,*
> *in the name of God the Father almighty who created you;*
> *in the name of Jesus Christ, Son of the living God, who suffered for you;*
> *in the name of the Holy Spirit who sanctified you;*
> *in the name of the glorious and blessed Virgin Mary, Mother of God;*
> *in the name of St. Joseph, her illustrious spouse;*
> *in the name of the Angels and Archangels, Thrones and Dominations, Principalities and Powers, Cherubim and Seraphim;*
> *in the name of the patriarchs and prophets, the holy apostles and evangelists, the holy martyrs and confessors, the holy monks and hermits;*
> *in the name of the holy virgins and all the holy men and women of God.*
> *May you rest in peace this day and your abode be in holy Zion;*
> *through Christ our Lord. Amen.*

"The beautiful soul of the zealous pastor of Holy Trinity took its flight to a better world 24 hours after Father Quémerais," as Mother Mary Hyacinth wrote to the novitiate in France just three days later.[219]

Father Biler returned to Fairfield at eleven o'clock that night, acknowledged that he was ill and told Mother Superior that he would telegraph his friend in Monroe for assistance the next day.[220]

In the confusion of the situation, many incorrectly believed that Shreveport was without a priest, not realizing that Father Biler was ministering in town and in Fairfield.[221] His sense of duty to return proved providential, for as soon as he reached town, he was summoned to the bedside of Sister Mary Martha, who had courageously answered Father Pierre's call for volunteers just a week prior.[222] The sister received Last Rites and slipped quietly into eternity at 2:00 a.m. As Mother recorded in the order's official register: "After four days of cruel suffering, she died at St. Mary's on 17 September, aged 47 years.…Her soul went to its Creator, rich with the merit of heroic charity in the service of yellow fever patients."[223]

Father Biler wrote a simple note at her bedside to be dispatched back to the motherhouse:

> + + *Sister Mary Martha died at 2 o'clock. See about digging the grave. If I can I will perform the burial at 11 o'clock this morning.*
>
> *Father Biler, Priest.*[224]

The brusqueness of the note did not betray a callous heart but revealed the magnitude of death surrounding the beleaguered Father Biler and the demands he faced. Father Biler arranged for a proper hearse, complete with pallbearers, for the procession to St. Vincent cemetery, with as much ceremony as could be mustered.[225]

At the convent, Mother Mary Hyacinth met with the sisters who could gather and used the context of *Laudes* (Morning Prayer) to inform them of Father Pierre's death. With no priest present that Ember Wednesday, there was no Mass. The sisters began their fast, and from within the convent chapel on the very land Father Pierre had secured for them, they again prayed the Office of the Dead for their benefactor. "*Regem, cui omnia vivunt, Venite adoremus*. The King, unto whom all things do live, come let us adore."[226]

As they were finishing the long prayer, their grief was compounded when Mother received the message from Father Biler of Sister Mary Martha's death.[227]

With the two of them now in their minds and hearts, they concluded their solemn prayer: "*De profundis clamavi ad te Domine, Domine exaudi vocem meam*. From the depths I have cried to thee, O Lord: Lord hear my voice…*Requiem aeternam dona eis*…Eternal rest give unto them."

†

Father Biler knew of someone he could count on for help: Father Louis Gergaud, part of the first group of missionaries to follow Bishop Martin to Louisiana. After committing the mortal remains of Father Pierre into the earth, Father Biler sent a telegram to Monroe:[228]

> *Louis Gergaud,*
> *I am alone here. Other priests of the city have died. Please come to my aid.*[229]

On the day the body of the beloved Shreveport pastor was lowered into the ground beneath the church he built, the *Times* openly declared itself reduced to nothing more than a public death record. On the front page appeared a column dedicated to news on the condition of notable fever victims. This column became a regular feature for issues to come, beginning on Wednesday, September 17. Solemnly recorded among the roll of the honored dead—and presented with the simple heading of "Catholic Priests"—was the death of Father Isidore Armand Quémerais, just twenty-six years old and yet a "very worthy priest." Father Pierre's death was not yet recorded.[230]

Father Quémerais died on the final day of the octave of the Nativity of the Blessed Virgin Mary, a day to reflect on her Seven Sorrows, a day known to the secular world as simply Monday, September 15, 1873. "Practicing the charity that immolates [Jesus Christ]," he died a martyr to his charity in the service of the sick and dying; and "the angels gathered him for heaven."[231]

Catholic Priests.

We regret to learn that Father Pierre is dangerously sick with the prevailing fever. Father Pierre has shown himself to be a host in this as well as former epidemics, and his death would be greatly deplored, not only by the members of his church, but by our community at large. His assistant, Father Quimerais, a very worthy priest, died on Monday.

Left: Father Louis Gergaud. *Courtesy of St. Matthew's Church, Monroe, Louisiana.*

Right: Death notice that appeared in the *Daily Shreveport Times*, September 17, 1873.

Detail of Father Isidore Quémerais, from the memorial stained-glass windows at Holy Trinity Church in Shreveport. *Authors' collection.*

The memory of Father Pierre inspired much charity, as he had in life. When Shreveport residents realized his genuine goodness, even representing a distinctly minority faith, he received "money in abundance" from those convinced he would use it prudently. Indeed, an inventory of his personal effects revealed he was virtually penniless. He gave away all he earned as offerings to the poor and to enhance the Church.[232] The bishop himself acknowledged him as "one of the most saintly priests" he knew in his many years of ministry.[233] The Shreveport Howard Association immediately passed a poignant resolution—the first of only a few—as a memorial of his tireless service and sacrifice to people in need.[234]

Detail of Father Jean Pierre, from the memorial stained-glass windows at Holy Trinity Church in Shreveport. *Authors' collection.*

The heroism of Father Pierre caused the *Times* to lament boldly. Its poignant *memorare* of his life filled nearly an entire column on the front page. The notice was the first that set aside the death of one individual from the simple rosters of the dead, given its own place in the annals of the epidemic. It was a true recounting of a life in the service of others.

†

One hundred miles east in Monroe, grasping the Western Union telegram, Father Gergaud knew there was only one response: "Am leaving by stage coach this evening."[244] The fifty-year-old French priest telegraphed his response immediately upon receipt of Father Biler's wire.

After nearly eighteen years as a priest, Father Gergaud had demonstrated himself to be a man of decisive action. In Monroe, he founded a parish among Catholics he described as "only in name and in Baptism." In his early days there, children pelted him with rocks in the streets.[245] One anti-Catholic physician in Monroe went so far as to purchase land next to Father Gergaud's small church and then erected an office that doubled as a nightly saloon, right up to the property line, just to annoy the priest. Yet Father Gergaud reserved his anger from the children and the adult anti-Catholics alike, using his considerable energy instead to turn a meager diocesan investment into a church, school and proper Catholic graveyard.[246]

Father Biler sent a similar plea to Bishop Martin in Natchitoches.[247] By that time, Father Biler knew his own life was slipping away, but the uncertainty of his last dispatch remained. Was it received in time? Would the bishop truly understand the gravity of need? Bishop Martin, mindful of the aid he gave in Baton Rouge to priests fleeing the fever in New Orleans years ago, was facing a shortage of priests before the epidemic. Now, even that number of clergy was dwindling quickly.

The Western Union worker in Monroe also served as village crier, as news of Father Gergaud's imminent departure swept town. Bishop Martin knew of Father Gergaud's successful ministry and thus had appointed him *Vicar Forane* for "all the districts situated between the Mississippi and Red River valley."[248] By 1873, Father Gergaud had established missions at nearby Homer, Columbia, Harrisonville and Woodville, the seeds of which would later mature into full parish communities, and the ministry in Monroe had grown tenfold under his leadership.[249]

The work had not been easy. In 1855, still early in his ministry in Louisiana, Father Gergaud wrote to his former bishop, Antoine Jacquemet of Nantes, describing many of the challenges he faced in northeastern Louisiana:

> *At Milliken's Bend...I did a lot of baptisms, blessed a few weddings, heard some confessions, and experienced some of the manners that our Protestant brothers use to address a Catholic priest, who must simply walk without taking into account the insults he is the object of, and be happy in his heart to be a little despised for the love of Jesus Christ.*[250]

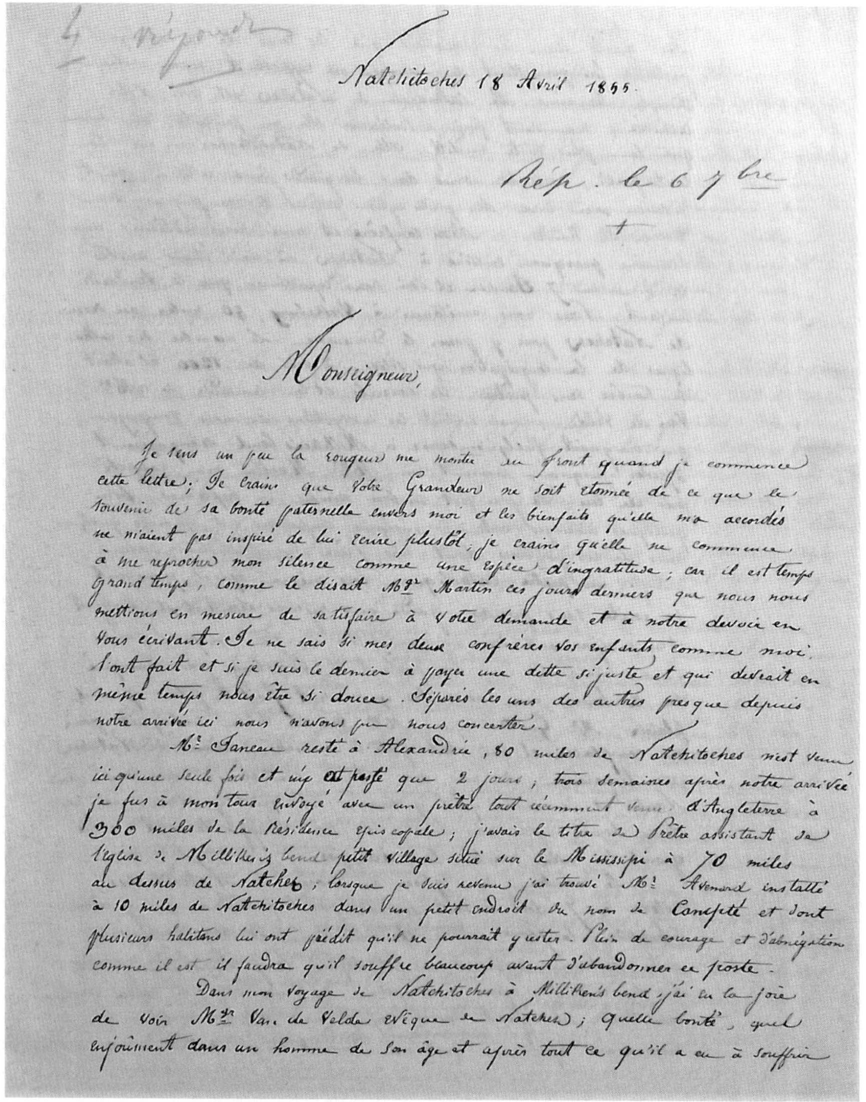

4 répondu

Natchitoches 18 Avril 1855.

Rép. le 6 7bre

+

Monseigneur,

Je sens un peu la rougeur me monter au front quand je commence cette lettre; je crains que Votre Grandeur ne soit étonnée de ce que le souvenir de sa bonté paternelle envers moi et les bienfaits qu'elle m'a accordés ne m'aient pas inspiré de lui écrire plustôt; je crains qu'elle ne commence à me reprocher mon silence comme une espèce d'ingratitude; car il est temps grand temps, comme le disait Mgr Martin ces jours derniers que nous nous mettions en mesure de satisfaire à votre demande et à notre devoir en vous écrivant. Je ne sais si mes deux confrères vos enfants comme moi l'ont fait et si je suis le dernier à payer une dette si juste et qui devrait en même temps nous être si douce. Séparés les uns des autres presque depuis notre arrivée ici nous n'avons pu nous concerter.

Mr Janeau resté à Alexandrie, 80 miles de Natchitoches n'est venu ici qu'une seule fois et n'y est resté que 2 jours; trois semaines après notre arrivée je fus à mon tour envoyé avec un prêtre tout récemment venu d'Angleterre à 300 miles de la Résidence épiscopale; j'avais le titre de Prêtre assistant de l'église de Milliken's bend petit village situé sur le Mississipi à 70 miles au dessus de Natchez; lorsque je suis revenu j'ai trouvé Mr Avenard installé à 10 miles de Natchitoches dans un petit endroit du nom de Campté et dont plusieurs habitans lui ont prédit qu'il ne pourrait y rester. Plein de courage et d'abnégation comme il est il faudra qu'il souffre beaucoup avant d'abandonner ce poste.

Dans mon voyage de Natchitoches à Milliken's bend, j'ai eu la joie de voir Mgr Van de Velde évêque de Natchez; quelle bonté, quel enjouement dans un homme de son âge et après tout ce qu'il a eu à souffrir

Original letter from Father Louis Gergaud to Bishop Antoine Jacquemet in France. *Courtesy of the Archives of the Diocese of Nantes.*

Father Gergaud's charity was likewise evident in the concern he expressed for the enslaved population, as he also lamented to Bishop Jacquemet:

> *The slaves are almost abandoned, and we cannot reach them right now, either because of the distrust of their masters, or because of the corruption*

> *that is pervasive here which makes it impossible to get into their camps without losing our honor and reputation.... The missionary priest to the slave and freedmen population Father Avenard*[251] *runs the risk of not having the opportunity to imitate the admirable devotion of Father Claver*[252] *to these people. Most of these poor souls are baptized, but for most of them, it is the only sign they have of a Christian.*[253]

As a Roman Catholic priest in a heavily Protestant area populated by many of the slave-owning planter class, his view to the evangelization of slaves likely contributed to the harsh treatment Father Gergaud received. He also contended with the Protestant opinions, as he penned to his former bishop in Nantes:

> *The only difficulties that our ministry encounters here are indifference, the love for pleasures and luxuries, and the lack of education, and all of this is enough to practice our zeal. In the north, the Catholic religion must handle and face attacks that remind me of the diatribes of Luther against the Papacy.*[254]

One evening, three men entered Father Gergaud's one-room abode uninvited as he finished his supper. Vienna sausage and French wine made up his staple meal and probably brought some comfort of home.[255] A liquored-up saloon patron from next door said to him directly: "Priest, we come to tell you that no one here sent for you....You must leave on the first boat, and if you don't, we'll make you."[256]

Father Gergaud rose deliberately and made a move for the closest man. The priest held back only a little: "Get out of here right now or I'll throw you out." The men left at once. Father Gergaud was never threatened in Monroe again.[257]

People also knew him for his generosity. In 1871, Father Gergaud expressed a desire to return to France to visit his mother, and the next week, prominent Monroe resident and former Civil War general John Frank Pargoud gave him a check for $500 to cover the cost. When a month passed and Father Gergaud had no travel plans, the general passed another check for the same amount, and this time, Father Gergaud agreed to spend the accumulated $1,000. He did not book an ocean voyage but instead purchased a square of land to begin St. Matthew's Cemetery. Thus grew the reputation of the character of this priest from Nantes.[258]

Now, as he prepared to board the six o'clock stagecoach for Shreveport, the locals begged him to remain in Monroe. Robert Ray, a local judge, remanded Father Gergaud, anticipating the appearance of yellow fever at Monroe any day. He said Father Gergaud would only end up abandoning his people when they needed him most. The good priest replied to the judge only, "It is my duty and I will go."[259]

Just a moment later, as he boarded the stagecoach, Father Gergaud whispered to his assistant pastor, the newly ordained Father Joseph Quelard: "Write to the Bishop. Tell him that I go to my death. It is my duty, and I must go."[260]

He then turned to the crowd and bade them all farewell. He told the coachman to drive on and looked ahead as the road drew him nearer to his final calling.[261] As Mother Mary Hyacinth wrote, "The noble Father Gergaud answered: 'I take the stage tonight.' What courage! What heroic devotion to a confrere!"[262]

Meanwhile, a third wave of relief arrived from New Orleans and brought news that the sickness was spreading on the vessels plying the river—where imprudence and greed were likely factors.[263] On September 19, E.F. Schmidt, the president of the New Orleans Howard Association, arrived with five additional nurses. Schmidt brought expertise, his philanthropist's heart and a passion to help others.[264] By the day after his arrival, there were 305 known deaths from yellow fever in Shreveport, not including dozens more who perished in outlying areas and neighboring towns.

The New Orleans Howards had already dispatched at least thirty-five physicians, nurses and druggists to Shreveport. Numerous other volunteers also entered through the semi-porous quarantine line.[265] The national publicity following the deaths of Fathers Pierre and Quémerais, as well as so many others, brought a sense of urgency to help. Father Gergaud now joined in the relief that this third wave offered.

Walking alone from the stage, Father Gergaud left all he knew behind. He voluntarily approached the city that many were fleeing.[266] Undoubtedly, he surveyed what was before him, taking in the landscape of his final earthly mission. There is perhaps no greater measure of charity than to think less of self than of others. Whatever crossed his mind that day, the certainty of his purpose propelled him forward.

In Another World

The black vomit returned—was copious & the case became hopeless. . . . I could not well bear the sight. . . . Taylor told me all was over. For some seconds I was in suspense feeling that the announcement was made to me in another world—that I was in another world.

—diary of Judge Henry Gerard Hall, September 22–23, 1873

Riverfront, Shreveport
Saturday, September 20, 1873
The Commemoration of St. Eustace and Companions, martyrs

Shreveport's shuttered storefronts, burning tar pits, muddy streets and moaning cries of the dying greeted Father Gergaud. He carried with him the history of his own homeland, where plague was common. Periodic epidemics remained a constant feature of life in Brittany, including the area around Nantes, the grand city of France's picturesque Loire River Valley. In 1832, the year of his birth,[267] France had a cholera outbreak with a shocking mortality rate of 25 to 50 percent. Over five thousand people died in Brittany alone. When he was sixteen years of age, another epidemic of cholera broke out, followed by yet another three years before his ordination in Nantes in 1854.

The rural environment of his childhood kept such outbreaks at a distance, as he grew up in a family of common laborers in the small village of Héric,

Héric, France, with St. Nicholas Church on right. *Authors' collection.*

sixteen miles north of Nantes. Héric was a hamlet born of the Middle Ages, as community clustered around farming of common lands. The sloping hills would have been verdant green in Father Gergaud's memory, due to an unusually rainy climate with mild summer temperatures. Louisiana had matched the rain, at least.

In Héric, the village cemetery reflected the town's medieval past, and among its dead were victims of plagues of the past, including bubonic plague, which ravaged all of France from the fourteenth through the sixteenth centuries. The local church dedicated to St. Nicholas had original foundations old enough to have witnessed the medieval pestilence. It was there the parents of infant Louis Gergaud presented him for baptism on the day following his birth,[268] in an eighteenth-century *église* that stood on

The Grand Seminary at Nantes, undated nineteenth-century postcard.

those older stones. He entered the Grand Seminary of Nantes on October 8, 1851, at the age of nineteen.[269]

Nantes had still-visible cobblestone and concrete evidence of the fourth-century Roman presence, and he could gaze on the stately Château des Ducs de Bretagne, with its thirteenth-century foundations. The manorial home of the dukes of Brittany was a constant reminder of the unique geopolitical identity of Nantes, at once fully French yet independent by centuries of association with historic Breton culture. The Grand Seminary had a long history stretching back to the early eighteenth century, before French Revolutionary radicals shuttered the seminary doors in 1793 and executed one of its Sulpician instructors who refused to turn over the keys.[270] The seminary reopened with the Bourbon restoration, and the young Louis Gergaud, a teenager during the 1848 revolution, knew well the bloody and tragic history of the Church in France. In Nantes, the Catholic landscape was unmistakable, its Gothic cathedral with a nave higher than that of Notre Dame in Paris and a cornerstone first laid in joint ceremony in 1434 by the bishop of Nantes and the duke of Brittany. Father Gergaud was steeped in this history.

It was the chapel of the Grand Seminary where the twenty-two-year-old Father Gergaud prostrated himself before Bishop Antoine Jacquemet and was ordained a priest of Jesus Christ on Saturday, September 23, 1854.[271] As his family and friends kissed his anointed hands after he offered them his first priestly blessing, Father Louis Gergaud knew that in less than a month's time, on October 21, he would leave his homeland, perhaps never to return.

From the cultural and architectural riches of Nantes, he journeyed to the missionary territory of Louisiana with its small wooden churches lacking ornamentation. Father Gergaud was a keen observer of such comparisons and contrasts, drawing on the memories of his homeland. Although he left behind a mild climate and magnificent cathedrals, Father Gergaud never ceased to find beauty and promise in his adopted Louisiana. As he once reflected in a letter to Bishop Jacquemet:

> *The Cathedral of Natchez (Mississippi) is far from completion, the outer structure is completed but the inside sadly lack signs of ostentation; the one in Natchitoches is the opposite—well ornamented, and during its grand church days, it could compete with any of the small churches we have in countryside of the Diocese of Nantes.*[272]

Thousands of miles from the Diocese of Nantes, when Louis Gergaud boarded the stagecoach in Monroe bound for Shreveport, any memories of France would have yielded no comparison. The stage road crossed flat cotton farmlands and a network of small streams and bayous that cut through pine forests. The rolling hills and pleasant temperatures of his homeland were in stark contrast to the Louisiana wilderness and humidity. The Loire River certainly had no rival in the Red River, aptly named for the muddy red-brown clay of north Louisiana.

It was this muddy river that formed the boundary of death-stricken Shreveport. What Father Gergaud saw was a town not unlike a medieval village in the grip of the Black Death. By September 20, most of the residents of means and influence were either dead, completely spent from exhaustion or were themselves down with yellow fever.

Every day must have seemed an Ember Day with fasting and works of mercy. This Ember Saturday, Father Gergaud went to find Father Biler and the sisters healthy enough that he took on other relief duties. He found the deathbeds of two former lay assistants of Father Pierre's parish and provided them with their Last Rites.[273] He also found a number of sick sisters and the nurses attending them. If it was still available, they received a strong dose of cathartic[274] and were encouraged to remain calm, simultaneously taking ice and repeating the Ave Marias of the rosary. Father Gergaud's presence

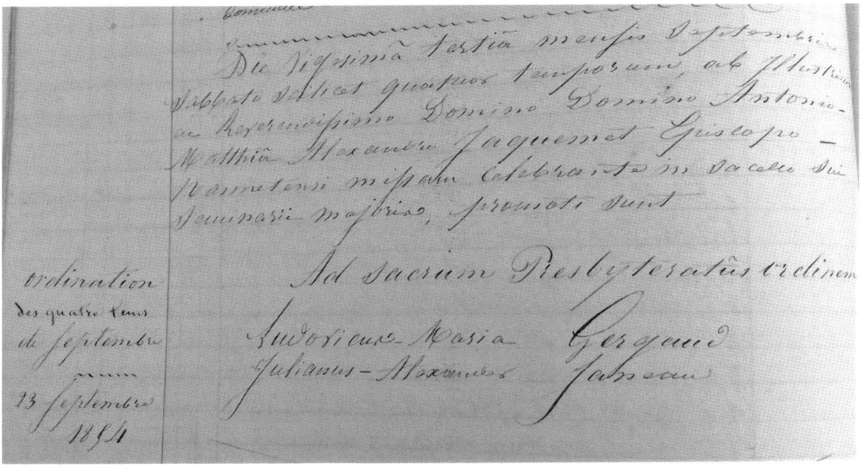
Die Vigesima tertia mensis Septembris Sabbato scilicet quatuor temporum, ab Illustrissimo ac Reverendissimo Domino Domino Antonio-Matthia Alexandro Jaquemet Episcopo Nannetensi missam celebrante in sacello Sui seminarii majoris, promoti sunt

ordination des quatre tems de septembre

Ad sacrum Presbyteratus ordinem

Ludovicus-Maria Gergaud

Julianus-Alexander Jahneau

23 septembre 1854

Ordination record of Father Louis Gergaud. *Courtesy of the Archives of the Diocese of Nantes.*

dispelled any fear that they would die without the sacraments. Certainly, they invoked the day's martyred saints, especially St. Eustace, one of the Fourteen Holy Helpers frequently invoked in medieval plagues.

Father Biler seemed to be improving at St. Mary's downtown, but this was part of the grim deceptive pattern of yellow fever.[275] Father Gergaud wanted him carefully moved back to St. Vincent's, where perhaps he would recover under the dutiful care of the sisters. On Sunday, September 21, Father Biler journeyed by enclosed carriage for a thirty-minute ride back to Fairfield, unaware that his second telegram, the one to Bishop Martin, had been answered. Father Le Vézouët would depart Natchitoches for Shreveport following the next morning's Mass. Upon Father Biler's arrival at the convent, the sisters rejoiced to see him again.[276]

Father Gergaud next turned to care for strangers. High on the list of victims were most certainly the volunteers themselves. He visited Otto Schnurr, the dry goods store clerk, who worked with Father Pierre and the first Howard volunteers in Fever Ward 1. Otto died the next day, having just reached his eighteenth birthday.[277]

As Father Pierre had the week before, Father Gergaud celebrated Sunday Mass, but there would be no church bells this time. All of the city's churches agreed to hold the sound of bells in reserve, belonging to a more accommodating time. This was another ominous parallel to fourteenth-century Europe, when towns also silenced local church bells, except for the single toll to announce the burial of the dead. Then, there had been no need of pealing bells, as fear of plague shuttered people in their cottages, isolating them from each other and the sacraments. In the depths of that September, it was clear that the bells in Shreveport would not ring again for some time, until they could ring in celebration at the close of an epidemic.[278] How soon could there be a frost?

As young Schnurr was laid to rest, the talk among the relief corps—now largely led by volunteers from New Orleans—was the widely publicized calculation that if the same outbreak, carrying the same mortality rate, were to strike the Crescent City, more than one thousand people would be expected to perish every day. This was a sobering calculation, indeed.[279]

Rain was a familiar constant companion, as unceasing as the grip of death around Father Gergaud. He splashed through the muck in his cassock ministering to the sick and the grieving and soon saw a member of his own home parish among the victims. James Muse Dabbs, residing at the Southern Hotel, on the south side of Milam Street between Market and Spring Streets, and now under the care of Dr. J.L. Brooks, worked in the stage office at the time of the outbreak and was now trapped by the Shreveport quarantine.[280]

Dabb's parents, Dr. Christopher Hunt Dabbs and Julia Washington Bourgeat Muse Dabbs, were among the closest friends Father Gergaud had in Monroe, sharing a close hospitality building St. Matthew's Church. They, like so many others, were moved by his generous heart, energetic nature, cultivated spirit and prudent and reserved manner.[281] Julia later taught in the first Catholic school founded in Monroe, St. Hyacinth's. Father Gergaud had baptized their two grandchildren, one of whom died hours after birth. Now, Father Gergaud visited with their son James, sharing the hope of Christ and as much time as he could at his bedside.[282] Later, as James penned a letter to his wife, yet another Howard volunteer, a young doctor, died of the fever. The ranks of the medical men were thinned yet again.[283]

Across town, at the home of Judge Henry Hall, his family lay clinging to life. The judge braved the rain and made multiple trips to the railroad depot to retrieve ice. Though weary, he sought distraction in sowing turnip seed in the yard—between his shifts caring for the sick—which, come harvest-time, he would be able to split with his hired help.[284]

Dr. Fenner arrived late one day and gave both patients an injection of some "oil" as Judge Hall looked on. Although the judge asked for further nursing assistance, he found little help over the coming days.[285] The death toll continued, and by the manner of his own writing, Judge Hall was shocked. Some of those he called on were too afraid to leave their homes—their own little quarantines within the great quarantine—not even to help the Hall family so desperately in need.

His family members were dehydrated and able to release only small amounts of urine of a dark reddish color, full of the noxious byproducts of the infection. An inability to pass urine was an ominous indicator.[286] The judge tried a combination of the medicines Dr. Fenner brought, including "bromide of potash" (potassium bromide), while he fed his wife and daughter ice chips and rubbed their foreheads with ice and cold compresses.[287] He stayed by their bedsides into the night, leaving the sick room only to tend his infant son who cried out during the night, wanting comfort from his now dying mother.

The judge ultimately lost the battle with his wife's fever. He was left alone with his two youngest children and wrote on the pages of what was once an ordinary journal of non-events:

> *Eugenia died about 9 o'clock at night....* [The] *black vomit returned—was copious & the case became hopeless. She became unconscious & altho* [sic] *the struggles & groans lasted long, I trust her consciousness of pain was not great. The effect on the nerves & muscles too was considerable, but perhaps not on sensation. I could not well bear the sight* [so I] *lay down between my little ones & lost consciousness till S.L. Taylor told me all was over. For some seconds I was in suspense feeling that the announcement was made to me in another world—that I was in another world.*

The next day, he buried his wife. Though advised to burn the bed she died in and all of her remaining earthly possessions, he would not; this chore he refused to obey.[288]

The Howard Association began pooling resources for more nurses and for an orphanage for the children of the dead. The surviving children, like those of the Hall family, found the broadly sweeping hand of death forever changed their innocent worlds. Many of those children had witnessed their parents' agony and burials, and this left an emotional toll. The fever proved especially prevalent, and disproportionately deadly, among younger adults and the middle-aged. The consequence was that within a few weeks, there were many orphans. The *New York Times* even reported on two traumatized siblings brought to the Howard's headquarters at the Board of Trade, eye-level with that green baize-covered table, on the night of September 21. Their relatives were all deceased, and they were completely alone in the world.[289]

The plight of one little girl also caught the attention of the local daily:

> *There is an orphan girl of ten or twelve years of age, being kept and cared for by one of the courtesans of the city at her house. The humanity some of the women of this class have displayed during the present epidemic…* [in nursing] *sick strangers…with care and tenderness, prompts the belief the woman has taken this child in kindness of heart and means well by her. Nevertheless it must be admitted the child is not in proper quarters.*[290]

At least some of the girls were eventually able to find a proper residence at the Poydras Female Asylum in New Orleans. The boys were largely on their own, reflecting greater acceptance of a boy growing up on the streets to fend for himself. In the interim, the Howard Association opened an orphan house in an abandoned residence in Shreveport during the last week of September, sheltering and feeding as much as two-thirds of the orphaned population of the city. After the orphanage was established, the Howard Association's operating expenses soared to about $2,000 per day.[291]

†

Tuesday, September 23, brought heat that pierced through the smoke hanging over Shreveport and burned up remaining rain puddles. The talk of the town was the high mortality rate among men of means throughout the business district. Since Shreveport owed its very existence to commerce, this seemed of great consequence. Still more talk included recognition that another distinct group was coming down with the fever—poor persons of color. Their bodies were also placed in the mass grave at the City Cemetery, dusted with lime and red clay, until someone else was in turn laid on top of them.[292] Among those latest corpses was that of Captain R.D. Sale of the Sale & Murphy mercantile, the headquarters of which was featured prominently in a photograph captured by Lieutenant Woodruff's lens taken during the onset of the epidemic.

Meanwhile, Father Gergaud introduced himself to Dr. Darwin Fenner, recently recovered himself from yellow fever, perhaps contracted during his struggle to keep Mrs. Hall and her children alive. The physician and the priest worked together for the next several days. Added to their number were a few locals who had at last recovered sufficiently to again volunteer. Prevailing medical theories of the day assured survivors of an immunity, at least from the mortal aspects of the disease. Those who survived were often sought to go into afflicted areas, and their presumed immunity often bore out in either no illness at all or a much milder course.[293] Two more replacement telegraph operators also arrived that week, one from Pensacola, Florida, and the other from Cincinnati, Ohio, to take up the indispensable machine and keep communications open.[294]

Also, rumors of "wild excitement" and a widespread crash on Wall Street, coupled with associated bank failures in Chicago, reminded Shreveport residents that the world outside had not stopped to wait for their recovery.[295] The Panic of 1873 temporarily wiped Shreveport off the front pages of the leading national newspapers. Few things steal headlines like major financial disaster.

As September neared its end, there was faint hope, even if due to morbid arithmetic. There were only so many people left alive. How many more could really be expected to die? The question seemed a logical one. Now, as October approached, the promise of frost was on the foreseeable horizon.

Removed from the conversations of morbid arithmetic or national financial troubles, Father Gergaud offered Mass on the anniversary of his priestly ordination. He surveyed the face of the fever's latest victim, Sister Mary Angela, and was able to administer the final sacraments in time. She died at St. Mary's at four o'clock in the afternoon of Tuesday, September 23, having answered the call from Father Pierre and her final calling in service to God. Father Gergaud paused in his relief efforts to accompany her mortal remains, with the customary psalms on his lips, back to St. Vincent's that evening.[296]

Sister Mary Angela was laid to rest in the convent cemetery, spared from the mass grave of the city. Sister Mary Angela (née Marie Angèle Le Nédélec circa 1835) came to Louisiana just four years prior and had only taken her final vows in August 1871, with Bishop Martin of Natchitoches presiding. Mother Superior assigned her to St. Mary's Day School in Shreveport for but a few months and later transferred her to Monroe. She then volunteered to come to Shreveport. Her course was typical, as she first exhibited signs of yellow fever on September 19 and died four days later.[297]

Father Gergaud, "a torch spreading light and heat around him,"[298] buried Sister Mary Angela himself, commending her soul to the Almighty at ten o'clock in the morning on Wednesday, September 24, a day in honor of Our Lady of Mercy. He then moved on to his next work of mercy, visiting the mourning sisters and Father Biler, who was in the "calm stage" and hopeful of recovery. His condition had worsened since the day before, when he was

able to sit up, write a few letters and "relish" the chicken prepared for him. When Mother Hyacinth checked on him at five o'clock in the morning, she found him with high fever and restlessness and sent for a doctor right away.[299] On the same Wednesday afternoon, September 24, both Fathers Biler and Gergaud took dramatic turns.

Father Gergaud suddenly collapsed about five o'clock that evening while caring for others, and at least two physicians tended to him. By then, the two priests were miles apart and without the ability to offer each other last

Opposite: Detail of Father Jean Marie Biler from the memorial stained-glass windows at Holy Trinity Church in Shreveport. *Authors' collection.*

Right: Father Francois Le Vézouët. *Image from prayer card.*

Below: The final resting place of Father Jean Marie Biler, moved from the Daughters of the Cross Cemetery to Forest Park Cemetery. The name inscription reflects the French variation of "LeBiler." *Authors' collection.*

sacraments. Father Biler passed through his "calm stage" and resigned himself to death. They could only await the arrival of the next priest to step into the breach.

The physician summoned to the convent early that morning arrived intoxicated. At Mother Hyacinth's insistence, Dr. Joseph L. Moore agreed to visit and assess Father Biler and the ill sisters. Dr. Moore advised that for Father Biler, it was too late, saying, "He has but a few hours to live."

Then came a minor miracle.

That afternoon, at the end of an arduous, four-day journey, Father François Le Vézouët passed through the convent's high-framed doorway to the bedside of Father Biler and, without delay, prepared to anoint and gave Holy Communion to his worthy confrere.[300] Father Biler, himself once filled with the spirit of the gallant relief corps, with no thought to his own safety or health—assisting countless others in their last moments and blessing their tombs[301]—now cried out, "I am going to Heaven! *Je vais au Ciel! Chan d'or Baradoz!*"[302]

A Tempest of Death

For six weeks the people of Shreveport have been in the midst of a tempest of death; hundreds of our people have been stricken down; many of our best, purest and most useful citizens have died.
—Daily Shreveport Times, *September 30, 1873*

Fever Mound, City Cemetery, Shreveport
Monday, September 29, 1873
Solemnity in Honor of St. Michael the Archangel

Evening rains eroded the thin layer of red clay covering the mass grave. The "stench arising from the decaying bodies" passed into the muddy streets below.[303] Physicians were concerned the gases would possibly spread disease. Yet there were few capable laborers available to cover the dead. Howard volunteers placed six new bodies in the grave on September 30, compounding the situation. Yet one of the latest corpses was not a victim of yellow fever.[304]

Late in the evening on Monday, September 29, a gang moved up Texas Street to the grocery owned by Leopold Baer, an early refugee from Shreveport, who met his own death from yellow fever in Marshall, Texas, on September 1. Among these men was Charles E. Pritchard, a twenty-nine-year-old printer and a married homeowner with an income that supported two children and a house servant. Three years before, he lived near Dr. Darwin Fenner and his family in the wealthiest section of Shreveport.[305]

Just one year earlier, he served as a constable of the city, but his name became associated with at least two scandals. One involved some questionable real estate deals, and the other charge was burglary—of which he was acquitted.[306] Just five months earlier, Pritchard was also charged with passing counterfeit bank notes.[307] Now, he and a gang of roaming bandits preyed on the quarantined district under curfew.[308]

Pritchard broke into Baer's grocery, and moments later, he lay dying from a gunshot—the discharge of a .32 pistol from a guard Baer hired before he fled Shreveport. Pritchard's swift fall from grace ended in the shallow end of the mass grave at the city cemetery.[309]

The editors of the *Times* followed the curious story of Charles Pritchard and his gang. After a complete reversal on the severity of the fever conditions, the local daily had become an invaluable way for city officials and the Howard Association to communicate vital information. The *Times* was also a tangible reminder of the Shreveport that existed before the epidemic. This last bit of daily normalcy was guarded at all costs. Every day, there was at least one certainty beyond more death notices: the paper kept printing news, the tiniest boosts to morale and a sense of newness to each day of monotonous death and despair.

On the day of Pritchard's burial, the final two agents of the newspaper became ill. There was an instant fear that Shreveport would become voiceless, causing irreparable harm to the city's reputation. Instead, "three yellow, feeble and emaciated convalescents" returned the next day to keep the paper publishing.[310] Newspapers across the country, including the *New York Times* and the *World* (also of New York), published an appeal from the Shreveport Howard Association for more funds and volunteers:

> *Our own resources are nearly exhausted. The wealthy are broken down, the poor are threatened with actual starvation, the sick and dying are about to be deprived of the commonest comforts humanity can offer them. We appeal not to our fellow-countrymen, but to our fellow-man for aid.*[311]

†

Father Le Vézouët found the sacred vessels and vestments where his deceased confreres left them in the sacristy of Holy Trinity. He was familiar with the church, as he had visited with some regularity between 1865 and 1871, even baptizing some of the parishioners' children from time to time.[312] He celebrated Mass outdoors on the Seventeenth Sunday after Pentecost. Those present heard the Last Gospel from Matthew 22 as Mass concluded, with Father Le Vézouët reading aloud the Greatest Commandment: "You shall love the Lord, your God, with all your heart, with all your soul, and with all your mind. This is the greatest and the first commandment. The second is like it: You shall love your neighbor as yourself."[313]

Following in the footsteps of his four confreres—Fathers Pierre, Quémerais, Biler and now Father Gergaud—there would be no rest for Father Le Vézouët, as he, too, lived out the greatest commandment. He spent the next few days in intermittent rain and continuous human peril moving from diseased, to dying, to deceased. He dutifully said his private Masses. On Monday, he did so at the bedside of his longtime friend Father Gergaud, whom he met at the Port of Le Havre in October 1854, with whom he traveled and shared meals those weeks on the Atlantic. Father Gergaud made the journey to Natchitoches for Le Vézouët's priestly ordination a year and a half after their departure from France.[314] Father Le Vézouët visited Monroe on at least one occasion, staying several days with his friend.[315] Suffering now with yellow fever, Father Gergaud could only listen as his friend offered Mass in honor of St. Michael the Archangel, praying for an end to the pestilence and imploring St. Michael's help.

The day after Charles Pritchard was placed in the mass grave, Father Le Vézouët began his fifth full day of ministering in Shreveport. On this day, he anointed the forehead and the backs of the hands of his dear friend. Father Gergaud's prophecy of his own death did nothing to hinder his zeal, nor did the pleadings of his own congregation as he left Monroe. In the midst of human suffering, Shreveport was a beacon for saintly acts. Now a charnel house of death and misery previously known for revelry, Shreveport became a place where Christian charity was on display, and observed, recorded and remembered by many.

Father Louis Gergaud relinquished his earthly struggle around half-past three in the morning on Wednesday, October 1.[316] The letter Bishop Martin hastily wrote the day before was too late. Having learned of Father Gergaud's decision to go to Shreveport, he wrote: "I beg you, my friend, to return to Monroe. Father Biler gave up his life. I have sacrificed dear Father Le Vézouët. That is enough, my God! That is enough!"[317]

Father Gergaud would not read this last imperative from his bishop. By the time the letter reached Shreveport, this *Homo Dei* had already sacrificed his life to charity. Shreveporters buried the beloved Monroe pastor near the young Father Quémerais in the City Cemetery.

Detail of Father Louis Gergaud from the memorial stained-glass windows at Holy Trinity Church in Shreveport. *Authors' collection.*

This heroic priest who had endured harassment from hostile non-Catholics in Monroe was never to know of an unsolicited remembrance published by a local Methodist pastor in the Monroe newspaper. It illustrates the admiration for the French priest:

> *He left Monroe, where he was in perfect safety, against the remonstrances of his friends, to go to Shreveport on a mission of mercy.... He knew his danger, but he knew his duty.... He fell in the battle—he fell as a noble man and Christian hero.... We can but love and admire a great man who adorns the Gospel as much as this man, and we sincerely hope, if we ever reach the Better Land, to find and know him there.*[318]

The body of Father Gergaud was later reinterred in St. Matthew's cemetery, which he founded in Monroe. The wording on his gravestone was chosen with precision to ensure that all who saw it would know that "he fell a martyr of his charity during the epidemic of Shreveport."[319]

†

On the day Father Gergaud died, Lieutenant Woodruff was laid to rest in the City Cemetery.[320] The *New York Times* reported to the world that Lieutenant Woodruff was likely to recover. The efforts of the Elstner family may have extended his life for hours or days, but Woodruff died on September 30 after a twelve-day battle with the cruel disease.[321] The people of Shreveport did not forget his valiant attempts at organizing relief and shelter for the afflicted. The local paper said of Woodruff: "He came among us about two years ago a perfect stranger, sent by his government to remove the raft in the Red River. By his courtesy to our people, stern integrity and unflinching industry and perseverance, he won the esteem of this community."[322]

Although four priests, two sisters, an army engineer and more than five hundred other children of God were already dead and buried, the first week of October brought hope with the arrival of an early cold front. For the survivors, a cool breeze blowing through the charnel house city must have seemed like the breath of God billowing through the dank streets. They hoped the "backbone of the monster" was now broken.[323]

A number of physicians were at the point of exhaustion, including Dr. Joseph Moore, who was battling yellow fever by late September and fully recovered to return to caring for the sick by early October. Among other medical men from across the region were Drs. Samuel Chopin, J.

A cartoon by artist Matt Morgan (1873) in *Frank Leslie's Illustrated Newspaper*, drawn during the yellow fever epidemic, depicts a victim in the clutches of a monster (Yellow Jack) with the figure of Columbia above pleading for help. *Library of Congress Prints and Photographs Division, Washington, D.C.*

Dickson Bruns and John Pintard Davidson. They arrived in Shreveport on September 25 to assess the situation and provide advice. They expected to return to New Orleans by early October, but the demand for their labors in Shreveport continued. By late September, each physician was tending to a minimum of forty patients each.[324]

Meanwhile, policing the beleaguered community became a challenge. Local authorities also suffered losses in their ranks, and criminal elements seized the advantage. Some were quite determined and were able to slip through quarantine to prey on the unfortunates within. On October 2, a notice was posted discouraging all "evil disposed persons" from pursuing "depredations" while the community was facing the epidemic. In complete frontier fashion, a posse of appointed gentlemen promised swift justice. This organized posse included L.R. Simmons, the president of the Shreveport Howard Association.[325] The city's self-policing by volunteer citizens only further reflects the desperate conditions.

Despite the promise of swift justice toward acts of "depredations," the very next day, thieves vandalized the cornerstone of a local church and stole the fifteen dollars placed inside a time capsule there. The bandits then carefully returned other mementos and documents they did not wish to steal. Thieves broke into the railroad depot the following evening, exchanging shots with a night watchman—all for a single sack of coffee that was ultimately left behind in the victimless gunfight.[326]

While vigilantes and thieves played a game of cat and mouse in the city, Shreveport's business leaders looked for the next steamer to arrive from New Orleans. River traffic had all but ceased. Red River packets *R.T. Bryerly*, *Frank Morgan* and *Royal George*, which just weeks before were common sights on the riverfront, were now at Baton Rouge. They later moved to within forty miles of Shreveport at Captain Robison's plantation and also at Coushatta, Louisiana, but their captains decided not to return to Shreveport until the fever relented. They sent word of this decision by telegraph and discharged their crews to work aboard other vessels in the interim.[327]

On the morning of October 3, a first Friday in honor of the Sacred Heart of Jesus, Father Le Vézouët showed the first telltale signs of yellow fever. He was the fifth priest to be stricken. He sent a plea to New Orleans for help, to ensure that Shreveport would have a priest to offer what only a priest could offer—the sacraments.[328]

The pleas from the priests came from concern for the physical needs of the city but, more importantly, that the sacramental life of the Church would continue. For them, it was the supernatural need that took priority. Their actions underscore an important aspect of their sacrifice. They understood that their work transcended earthly existence; therefore, their most important concern was the care of the suffering but eternal souls awash before them—even at the cost of their own lives.

God Help and Relieve Them

This terrible fever in Shreveport is fourfold worse.
From our inmost heart we can only say, God help and relieve them.
—Daily Picayune, *New Orleans, September 28, 1873*

Residence of the Archbishop, New Orleans
October 3, 1873
The Feast of St. Wenceslaus, duke, martyr

The same Father James J. Duffo, SJ, of New Orleans, who assisted the new Bishop Martin when he journeyed home in 1854 to recruit missionary priests, was an obvious choice to respond to Shreveport. During the 1853 yellow fever outbreak in New Orleans,[329] the young Jesuit slept on a cot in his church rectory to be available to answer calls for help at once, to miss no faint cry for help and to bring *viaticum* to the dying. His fellow Jesuits considered him "a man of iron constitution and dauntless courage."[330]

The sixty-eight-year-old archbishop of New Orleans knew these things, too. Napoléon-Joseph Perché, a native of Angers, France, who had served the Church since 1837, received a message from a desperate priest in Shreveport. The need was great, but who to send? By now, the heavy price a volunteer should expect to pay was well known.[331]

Bishop Martin of Natchitoches had no other priests to spare. Four were dead of yellow fever, and the fate of his trusted protégé and many sisters and laity hung in the balance. Bishop Martin may have believed he had sent them to their deaths, but these were deaths that gave them opportunity to achieve a rare sanctity. Bishop Martin requested that the archbishop send only priests with prior yellow fever experience—and hopefully "immunity." The priests were Fathers Duffo, SJ, and Charles S.M. Férec, a curate of the famed St. Louis Cathedral.[332]

Just two days before Fathers Duffo and Férec left for Shreveport, a New Orleans paper declared the yellow fever epidemic there to be "fourfold worse" than anything seen by the infamously unhealthy Crescent City in decades. "God help and relieve them," the editors pleaded.[333] Unlike the five before them who accepted a certain death—so sacrificial in nature—Fathers Duffo and Férec thought themselves immune.

When they arrived in Shreveport, they found a shocking cross-section of human behavior. There were thieves at work, matched by the vigilante posse. There were orphans left alone to beg for shelter, food and attention. A new wave of walking convalescents, the survivors of late September, were again joining the land of the living as they left their would-be deathbeds behind.

Many flocked to the Mechanic's Exchange building, where a local philanthropist, Henry Dillenburger, served fresh, hot soup to recovering victims, regardless of their ability to pay. Still others came out simply to clear the record and remove their names from the long rolls of the presumed dead. Meanwhile, the Shreveport Howards sent a foraging party across the Red River, effectively breaking the quarantine. Many of those not infected were on the brink of starvation. Chicken was in particular demand, especially for soup believed to be medicinal. The foraging party found little besides more sick to the east, indicated in reports of several "violent" cases. This exacerbated fear that the epidemic was spreading beyond the quarantine, and not lessening, and this expedition returned to Shreveport in haste.[334]

†

"Jesus then said to the paralytic, 'Rise, pick up your stretcher, and go home.' He rose and went home. When the crowds saw this they were struck with awe and glorified God."[335] That passage from the Gospel of Matthew no doubt echoed in the mind and heart of Father Le Vézouët on Sunday, October 5, following what would be his final Mass. The pastoral responsibilities he left behind were manifold. There were missionary churches he established across the western periphery of the diocese and the loving bond he formed with the Spanish Creoles living in the hinterlands near the Sabine River, the old borderland with Texas. There, he had converted many common-law marriages into valid sacramental unions and brought the sacraments to a remote, poverty-stricken and largely forgotten people. He was both a "father" and a friend, a source of encouragement and consolation.

Among his last duties, Father Le Vézouët provided Rose of Lima, a young novice who would never take the veil, with her final sacraments. Sister Mary of the Cross, Sister Mary Loretto and Sister Seraphine were all also ill with the virus, as was Mother Mary Hyacinth.[336] Nearly all of the remaining Catholic community was ill, waiting for the next priest. The thought of dying without the sacraments was impossible to contemplate, as Mother Hyacinth wrote of this possibility: "Now only Father Le Vézouët is left in Shreveport. If he succumbs, we will die without the sacraments. *Fiat! Fiat! Fiat!!*"[337] Mercifully, the young novice Rose would be the final Daughter of the Cross to perish, although many contracted the disease.

Overcoats and shawls were pulled out of trunks and armoires as strong winds blew, bringing what Louisianans deemed cold weather. Still, the physicians warned absent residents not to return to Shreveport behind the front of cold air until health officials declared the epidemic over.[338] National interest stirred again with sensational coverage by the leading New York periodical, *Frank Leslie's Illustrated Newspaper*. No longer distracted by the financial panic, the paper reminded its readership of the human suffering in Shreveport, with illustrations that were nothing short of haunting.

One etching depicted a deserted townscape, save for a hearse and two carriages of mourners following to City Cemetery, the most common scene by day. Another etching showed a fumigated Texas Street, with dense clouds of black smoke with pyres set at regular intervals. The plight of the telegraph operators, working themselves to the point of death, was also captured in accurate detail. Also illustrated was the "family hospital," the room of a well-furnished house where a young girl played, stacking cards, while surrounded by shrouded bodies of her family. Her house of cards was soon to tumble around her. This was a typical ending to countless Shreveport stories.

Back on the front lines of the epidemic, the newspaper continued to warn: "Rascals and scoundrels of the country…anxious to take advantage…of our afflicted condition, and prey upon us….There is manliness enough left in Shreveport to resent all insults; to spurn with contempt all affiliation with scoundrels, and to severely punish all depredators!"[339]

Following the September exodus and hundreds of resident deaths, there were probably fewer than one thousand healthy people remaining. A short-

OCTOBER 4, 1873.] FRANK LESLIE'S ILLUSTRATED NEWSPAPER. 57

VIEW OF THE LEVEE, SHREVEPORT.

FUMIGATING THE TOWN—A SCENE IN TEXAS STREET.

THE TELEGRAPH OFFICE—"GOOD-NIGHT."

LOUISIANA.—THE YELLOW FEVER EPIDEMIC AT SHREVEPORT.—FROM PHOTOGRAPHS AND SKETCHES BY CHRISTIAN OLSEN.

Above and opposite: Etchings from *Frank Leslie's Illustrated Newspaper*, New York, October 4, 1873. *Authors' collection.*

lived but discernible frost appeared on the ground in scattered patches of low places across the city. It was a welcomed sight on the morning of Tuesday, October 7. Many of these patches were the same puddled areas where the last wave of mosquito larvae hatched.

James Muse Dabbs wrote to his family in Monroe of the joy of the frost. Yet he also wrote of his increasing despair at being separated behind the quarantine and away from his wife for so long: "We had a light frost.... You don't know how I miss you these cold nights. I'm tired of this kind of life and when we get together I hope I will never have to leave you so long again." Unlike his beloved pastor, Father Gergaud, James Dabbs recovered, although he lost more than twenty pounds from his body.[340]

THE HOUSEHOLD HOSPITAL—THE LAST OF THE FAMILY.

Those who heard of Father Le Vézouët's condition despaired. Not conscious of the morning's frost, the fifth French father was on his certain deathbed, even though the local paper, in typical fashion, spread hope he would recover.[341] Two of his nurses, hired Howard Association men, L.V. Coiron and R.G. Wiltz, from New Orleans, were with him on October 8.[342] With prayers of faithful nuns pounding on heaven's door, Father François Le Vézouët, wanting only "the surest and shortest path to heaven," was dying violently, as if his own Good Friday before Easter Sunday, expelling black vomit in his last hours.

Through divine mercy personified, the New Orleans priests Duffo and Férec arrived at Father Le Vézouët's bedside—visiting him literally as their first patient on duty in Shreveport. There were mere moments to spare. Father Le Vézouët, fearful of dying without the sacraments, was found to have a pix with the Blessed Sacrament around his neck. With heroism that surpassed even his missionary zeal, the saintly priest passed quickly thereafter, yet one more martyr to his charity.[343]

Father Le Vézouët died at the residence of Dr. Joseph Moore on Fairfield Avenue, north of the convent. Dr. Moore was Father Le Vézouët's primary medical caregiver and himself a Catholic convert, as his family was listed among those who received the sacrament of Confirmation at Holy Trinity a dozen years earlier in 1861.[344]

Detail of Father François Le Vézouët from the memorial stained-glass windows at Holy Trinity Church in Shreveport. *Authors' collection.*

Thus, the New Orleans priests were initiated into the confraternity of charnel house priests. The confreres faced dual missions: to bring hope and peace to dying strangers, and to continue the Catholic sacraments for the remaining faithful. Yet, in the bold face of all that is good, the forces of darkness were still at work. After Father Le Vézouët's death, thieves stole his watch, crucifix and other personal items from his body. The two suspects were none other than two Howard nurses, Coiron and Wiltz. The posse detained them, but without sufficient evidence, they forcefully took the suspects to the edge of the quarantine and told them to leave at once.[345]

Bring Along Their Coffins

Absentees should not be in any hurry to return, but if they insist, we advise those of a speculative turn to bring along their coffins as the stock is about exhausted and prices are enormously high. They will save time and money by it.
—Daily Shreveport Times, *October 22, 1873*

Caldwell Livery and Stables, Fever Ward 1
Thursday, October 9, 1873
The Feast of Sts. Dionysius, Rusticus and Eleutherius, martyrs

To the morbid delight of the editors of the *Daily Shreveport Times*, Caldwell Stables unveiled a "magnificent" new hearse.[346] Received a week earlier by special order, the grim carriage drew quite a crowd. The Clarence Glass Hearse made its way to Shreveport by a circuitous route aboard either the Marshall supply train or the steamer *Bertha*. The latter, a recent arrival from Opelousas, Louisiana, with its captain flaunting the quarantine, was the first steamboat to land at Shreveport in many days. The arrival of a river steamer was likely an occasion for celebration, even if chief among its cargo was a grand conveyance of the dead. This day's edition of the *Times* reported that the lavish carriage was the finest ever seen in that part of the South and cost the investors $2,500 to manufacture.[347]

A Clarence Glass Hearse, circa 1870s, such as the one that arrived in Shreveport in early October 1873. *Courtesy of the Ohio History Museums.*

Cash was scarce in the city as the impact of the epidemic hit economically. For weeks, the Howards had relied on hired help, alongside volunteers, including the Catholic clergy and religious. By October, the organization faced an exodus of exasperated unpaid nurses. The loss of paid medical personnel spelled potential disaster, so the Howards posted an impassioned plea for the reconsideration of its near-mutinous paid staff in the local paper.[348]

Another 110 burials were recorded in the first two weeks of October, while no "hard freeze" to truly kill off the disease was forecast.[349] The *Times* projected on October 10 and 11 that Shreveport could expect to suffer for at least another month if the temperatures remained at the current average.[350] Because one popular theory suggested yellow fever outbreaks lasted approximately ninety days, the paper mused that the disease "will have to draw on us sparingly over the next thirty seven days, or the material will not hold out."[351] With no end in sight, the experienced New Orleans physicians, headed by Dr. Samuel Chopin, again announced their intention to return south as soon as possible.

By Sunday morning, October 12, at least 599 City Cemetery burials had been recorded since the epidemic began. Approximately half of the population remained in self-imposed exile, awaiting the time when the distant ringing of church bells would signal it was safe to return home.[352] On this Sunday, Mass was again held outside. While signing himself with the cross, the Jesuit proclaimed in a loud voice: "*Salus pópuli ego sum, dicit Dóminus: de quacúmque tribulatióne clamáverint ad me, exáudiam eos*.…I am the salvation of the people, says the Lord. In whatever tribulation they shall cry to Me, I will hear them."[353]

Burglaries remained a threat to civil order. Crime in the area indicated the destabilizing social effects of the epidemic and highlighted the lack of reliable civic institutions. A grieving widow, whose husband had only recently succumbed, managed to stop a particularly fiendish wretch from forcing himself on her. Although she fought him off, he was able to flee the city, as the posse could spare no manpower to bring him to justice.[354]

Payday finally arrived with great relief, and the Howard Association's hired nurses and doctors received their salaries, including past-due wages, on Tuesday, October 14. While jokes circulated that the payday gathering at the Mechanic's Exchange Building was the largest crowd seen since the beginning of the epidemic, certainly no one forgot that at least fifteen Howard Association volunteers, not including the paid caregivers, had perished by mid-October.[355]

Judge Henry G. Hall was among the Howard Association's latest patients to succumb to the fever. After his wife's death, he nursed two of his young children back to health before himself dying of the fever on October 15. Among the final entries of his poignant diary, he wrote: "I felt a little chilly at the feet once or twice today, but am still quite well tonight. I feel hopeful that I may escape the fearful plague, & I humbly pray to God that I may be spared awhile for the sake of my children."[356] Judge Hall spent his last conscious hours helping a Howard Association nurse, whom he described as sent "by the blessed Savior Himself" to bring his young son Henry back to health.[357] Henry awoke an orphan—that common Shreveport scenario captured by the *Frank Leslie's* illustrator.

With untold joy, news arrived that afternoon that President U.S. Grant had dispatched rations to Shreveport from the army's stock.[358] No organized disaster aid system was in place for such a response of the federal government, and this executive action spoke directly to the priority of Shreveport and to the efficacy of the *Frank Leslie's* national coverage.

Yellow fever did not discriminate by class or race. Yet concern arose after the death of Sam Peters, the cashier of the Freedman's Savings House and Trust Company of Shreveport, who was also a member-elect of the Reconstruction-era Louisiana congressional delegation. Peters was well-liked and respected by both Blacks and whites and successfully navigated the perilous line of acceptance by the white community and simultaneous trust from the Black community. His sudden passing left many of the formerly enslaved population in relative unease. Within the Freedman's Bank, there was on deposit more than $50,000 in liquid assets, possessions and real estate titles belonging to the Black people of Shreveport—four times the amount recorded just ten years earlier but still less than 1 percent of Shreveport's total wealth.[359]

Nervous residents holding deposits began to gather daily outside the bank, which remained locked, with no staff remaining after Sam Peters's death. He left no instructions or combination to open the bank's safe. Suspicions rose among both the Black and the white communities that someone may try to forcefully enter the bank and seize the currency. Black citizens sought to guard their own savings from the thieves preying on the city. If white thieves robbed the Freedman's Bank, then people who lost money would have virtually no recourse. There was also growing speculation that the reserves of the bank were tied in with national losses in the ensuing financial crisis of the month before.[360] Mercifully, no acts of violence came from the Freedman's Bank standoffs, but it underscores the tensions wrought by the epidemic to every aspect of society.

Father Duffo immersed himself in the care of the newly orphaned, at the mercy of whoever would take them. At least two New Orleans orphanages promised to take the children, but only after the threat of fever had abated. Father Duffo solicited and received financial assistance to establish a temporary children's home in Shreveport. Just two months earlier, families were sharing houses because accommodations were so scarce; now there was an abundance of empty dwellings, and it became the Jesuit's task to find suitable lodging to rent for those orphaned.[361]

From a distance, Bishop Martin worried over the status of his ailing diocese. In a letter dated October 14 written to Father Joseph Gentille, the rector of St. Patrick's in Lake Providence in the extreme northeast part of the state, Bishop Martin's desperation to cover the sacramental needs of his flock was obvious. The letter also reflected the fluid nature of news at his disposal, including an apparent lack of confirmation that Father Le Vézouët was dead from yellow fever:

> *You will of necessity have to go to either Shreveport or Monroe. I would prefer that you go to Shreveport for several reasons, yet give me freely your opinion in this matter. I can do nothing before the end of November, when the plague will have ceased, and Father Le Vézouët having returned, if the*

> *news of his death be not confirmed, I will be able to confer here with my Council in order to decide what to do.*[362]

Approximately two weeks later, on October 31, the bishop again wrote to Father Gentille confirming the arrangements for Shreveport, understanding that Father Duffo's presumed immunity made him a natural choice to remain. Bishop Martin delayed the appointment of Gentille as the new pastor of Holy Trinity until the epidemic completely abated. As he wrote: "Father Duffo will remain in Shreveport until the middle of December, for at that time all the danger will have passed. This will be the time specified for your arrival."[363]

On the Feast of St. Luke, October 18, Father Duffo met in the church office for a "mixed religion marriage" and, having the promises of both parties to raise the children Catholic, "joined in the bonds of matrimony Charles Gunter, son of John Frederick S. Gunter and of Mary Elizabeth Gunter… and Catherine Woods, daughter of Edward Woods and of Mary Murphy." He duly signed the marriage registry, as was his fashion, "J.J. Duffo, S.J." This first celebration of matrimony since Father Pierre's last wedding on September 1 brought a moment of joy to the small Catholic population. There was a beacon of hope cutting through the grim shadow of death.

On the morning of October 20, a more substantial frost formed. Survivors dared to muse that the grip of the fever was beginning to wane. Steamboat captains sent telegrams ahead, promising to return commerce to the city soon. The local daily resumed its usual attacks on the mayor and the administration for their inability to remove dead cats from the city streets or repair wooden foot bridges over open cesspits that presented a public hazard.[364]

Businesses reopened in the "lower" portion of the city along the riverbank, and despite the public fanfare, the lavish glass-paneled hearse at Caldwell Stables was now rarely seen.[365] Street traffic returned in the form of simple farm and passenger wagons, now moving foodstuffs rather than corpses or tar barrels. The survivors, emboldened by the thinnest veil of frost that burned up almost as quickly as it appeared, came out from their personal quarantines, perhaps prematurely. A handful of residents continued to die with each day that passed, and physicians remained cautious. It was no time for the refugees to return home. They were given this glib warning: "Absentees should not be in any hurry to return, but if they insist, we advise those of a speculative turn to bring along their coffins as the stock is about exhausted and prices are enormously high. They will save time and money by it."[366]

The robbery of Father Le Vézouët's corpse of his crucifix and watch came again to the public forefront when the New Orleans *Daily Picayune* published a claim of innocence from the suspects Coiron and Wiltz that was reprinted in the Shreveport paper. The men sought to clear their names after barely escaping Shreveport with their lives.[367] The nurses who had cared for the saintly priest requested that all concerned parties inquire of Fathers Duffo and Férec, who knew them and would attest to their innocence.[368] Nothing further is known of the incident, but the reappearance of this event in the public eye gave grateful citizens the opportunity to speak again of the heroic Father Le Vézouët. To take advantage of a visiting Catholic priest who was in town only to help the suffering—at the cost of own life—was too much for anyone's conscience.

As the leaves of the hardwoods along the river dried and dropped silently to the earth, the fever concentrated in the outlying rural districts, on the hills and in the lowland environs. The pestilence continued finding the hiding places of Shreveport's refugees, the homes of the landed planter and the humble sharecropper, the shacks of the river rat and the log homes of the subsistence farmer, as equally suitable places to wreak its havoc. Marshall, Texas, the origin of the weekly relief train, also was suffering from its own outbreak. One Shreveport physician volunteered to help in Marshall and noted that of seventy-one people under his care, forty-nine ultimately perished from the disease. The Shreveport Howard Association began to organize relief efforts and hire nurses for Marshall on October 22, wishing to return their generosity. As the Howards were shifting their focus, a late evening wind blew in yet another cold front. Then a dampening rain set in, the type that normally sparked health concerns, but this year, the approach of winter was welcomed.[369]

After two difficult weeks, Father Férec became ill with the fever.[370] His illness came as little surprise to anyone, as the priests were constantly laboring in their care of the sick. The Catholic clergy mortality rate was then 100 percent, and two Daughters of the Cross sisters and one novice had also died. Father Duffo found himself in a familiar situation, a parallel to the 1853 yellow fever epidemic in New Orleans, where he alone ministered in the neighborhoods near the Jesuit house. Then, Father Duffo had enjoyed an immunity that now remained apparent in Shreveport.[371] Fortunately, Father Férec recovered quickly.[372] As a resident of New Orleans, Father Férec probably did have some natural immunity, which possibly explains his less complicated course.

As Father Férec was regaining his strength, the familiar river steamer *Frank Morgan* passed by the commercial district on its way to Jefferson, Texas, on Thursday morning, October 23. The vessel did not stop at Shreveport but slowed long enough to drop a barge of goods, pushing the unmanned raft toward the riverbank. Men pulled the ropes and brought the barge to land. This was another nod to Shreveport's eventual return to normalcy, only the second sign of commerce the starving city had seen in weeks.[373]

GLAD TIDINGS

There was not much business doing yesterday, but there was some of the tallest kind of getting about, looking after ice, and then circulating the glad tidings.... Many persons visited [the ice just] *to satisfy themselves of its presence.*
—Daily Shreveport Times, *October 29, 1873*

HOLY TRINITY CATHOLIC CHURCH, FEVER WARD I
SUNDAY, OCTOBER 26, 1873
TWENTY-FIRST SUNDAY AFTER PENTECOST

Father Duffo's Sunday Mass was the first indoor public church service in weeks. At 8:00 a.m. on October 26, the Jesuit celebrated Mass *inside* the church Father Pierre built and, on behalf of all present, offered the prayer used on this Sunday each year since the end of the eighth century: "*Famíliam tuam, quǽsumus, Dómine, contínua pietáte custódi: ut a cunctis adversitátibus, te protegénte....*Guard your family, we beseech you, O Lord, with continual mercy, so that it may be free from all adversities as You are protecting it."[374]

Father Férec, still recovering at the Fairfield convent, offered Mass that twenty-first Sunday after Pentecost with the remaining sisters, many of whom remained ill. St. Mark's Episcopal Church, with its rector, Reverend Dr. William Dalzell, also announced a Sunday service at eleven o'clock that morning.[375] The spiritual life of the city was returning.

The offering of the first indoor Holy Mass signaled stabilization of the community. By this unseasonably cool Sunday morning, fewer people were becoming ill, while many more had begun to recover. Stores were beginning to reopen. Yet despite the influx of monetary donations and goods received from the relief train, the epidemic had consumed so much capital and materials that very little business could actually be conducted.[376] There were but three yellow fever burials in the City Cemetery on that hope-filled Sunday.[377]

The following Monday, the *R.T. Bryerly* arrived from Jefferson, Texas, and docked at the ferry landing. The vessel discharged its freight and remained in the channel across from Shreveport until departing the next morning for New Orleans to reload. The once routine event was now a perfectly symbolic moment announcing the return to normalcy.[378] Eight south Louisiana nurses and one physician, all returning home to New Orleans, were onboard, along with cotton, cattle and other common Shreveport exports.[379] Riverboat trade, the life engine of the city, had returned.

The rhythm of normal life unashamedly returned more and more, as did the daily offering of Mass with its inherent mystery. At each Mass, Fathers Duffo and Férec prayed for the deceased, especially their brother priests, recalling the offering of their lives. They offered the Votive Mass *in tempore mortalitatis* for the deliverance in time of pestilence. "In Thy clemency withdraw the scourge of Thy wrath."[380] They called on the Communion of Saints whose feast days the Church commemorated that October, martyrs and confessors, a virgin and a widow. Later they prayed through the intercession of an archangel as well.

Shreveporters broke into a rush of unfettered emotion on the morning of Tuesday, October 28, when they awoke to find "plentiful" ice filling the chug holes, rutted and lime-laced streets and drainage ditches of the city. The ice lasted well into the mid-morning—even in the most exposed places. The weather then remained clear but cold. Shivering Shreveporters met one another in the streets again. Jubilation ensued at the prospect of continued life for themselves, for their loved ones, for their city. They proffered "glad tidings" to one another and celebrated with "a gayful countenance brimful of hope!" The lost priests and sisters had once comforted the same people who now wrapped themselves in overcoats and shawls and carried on with life, celebrating the epidemic's end. A mercifully early frost had arrived.[381]

The physicians convened to discuss the fortunate change in the weather. Would it last long enough to kill off the pestilence? Would a warm change bring the disease back? Was this really the end of the horror? Ultimately, they

The steamboat *R.T. Bryerly* on the Red River. *Library of Congress Prints and Photographic Collection, Washington, D.C.*

proclaimed Shreveport *safe* from the period of nine o'clock in the morning until sunset each day.[382] It was clear to all that an end to Shreveport's isolation was forthcoming.[383]

Fathers Duffo and Férec shifted their focus toward ministering to a traumatized and mournful flock. Father Duffo baptized Anna Ritter, the five-week-old daughter of John and Mary, now that her parents no longer feared the disease. It had been many weeks since Father Isidore Quémerais performed the last recorded baptism on St. Lawrence's feast day, August 10. The routine of the priests now included meeting with parishioners and many others in shock, grieving, recovering and those still dying. The efforts of the Shreveport Howards now focused on expending the last of their resources on the recovering poor. Their purchases from the local merchants and freight from the river packets helped rejuvenate the local economy. To those who feared Shreveport could never recover "her prestige and progressive impulse," the editors of the *Times* included a long column of upbeat words: "We trust that our people will rise out of their despondency, look at the situation in its true light and renew with redoubled vigor and fresh hopes

The Situation

Is evidently improving daily. The reports from the sick yesterday were generally favorable, and we heard of no new cases. This is a point gained. Our city yesterday presented a more business like appearance, than at any time this season. There were a good many refugees in town, as well as a large number of residents from the immediate vicinity. Most all of the stores were open, and there was more or less business doing in a small way. There was a heavy run on the Howard charity store by the black people, and fears were entertained that it would suspend before night. It is the general impression that the quarantine against us and the Texas and Pacific railroad will be raised during the coming week, when active business will be inaugurated.

From the *Daily Shreveport Times*, November 2, 1873.

the conduct of their business."[384] Like the medieval *rota fortunae* (wheel of fortune), Shreveport's fall from a commercial high to a dismal low was now finally spinning in its favor, ascending from misery to prosperity.

On the evening of Thursday, October 30, the Howard Association hosted two physicians from Dallas, Texas, whom they entertained with a banquet dinner. Largely a political show, the gathering was to reinforce the positive message of a return to health. The Howards struck at the primary topic right away: was the medical community ready to approve the lifting of the quarantine and open the city again to the outside world?

The quarantine was indeed lifted with a proper resolution complete with a litany of *whereas* statements and a cadence of growing vigor that closed, directly: "Resolved, That a committee of the members of the medical profession of the city of Shreveport, respectfully recommend…it is perfectly safe to renew our social and commercial relations with the outside world."[385] Surely, the church bells of Shreveport rang out in harmonious celebration.

On the last page of the interment list of victims of the yellow fever epidemic of 1873, the Howard Association inscribed the names of the final thirteen who died.[386] These unfortunates, who died in the first ten days of November, became ill just before the hard frost, which lasted several days following its first sustained appearance on October 28. The last of the virus-propagating *Aedes aegypti* mosquitoes were now dormant due to the temperature change. Accordingly, the *Times* began referring to the aftermath of what they had termed "the Epidemic" and "the Plague" as simply "the Situation" on Sunday morning, November 2. As the paper proclaimed, "The situation is evidently improving daily. The reports from the sick yesterday were generally favorable, and we heard of no new cases. This is a point gained."[387] For the first time in seventy days, there were no burials of yellow fever victims to record.

†

On Monday morning, the catafalque, draped by a long black pall, stood before the altar, along with six silver candlesticks and unbleached candles. Above them all rose the tall Paschal candle, a flame burning in the memory of the dead, with the hope of the Resurrection. That Paschal candle was first lit 205 days before, for the Easter Vigil on April 12, by the ever-mourned Father Jean Pierre—whose earthly remains, next to Father François Le Vézouët's, lay freshly buried beneath the floor of the sanctuary. This beloved pastor whose own flame was snuffed out too quickly was buried in a substantial iron casket and interred near the high altar of the church he built.[388]

As November 2 fell on Sunday that year, the All Souls Mass was offered instead on Monday, with more people gathered than usual. Like any Requiem Mass, it began and ended with the same words: *Requiem. Requiem æternam dona eis, Domine: et lux perpetua luceat eis.* (Eternal rest grant unto them, O Lord: and let perpetual light shine upon them.) As the Paschal candle illuminated the black-draped representation of a coffin, and as Father Duffo read the epistle, the gathered faithful surely reflected on the many lives lost to the epidemic, on the five priests and others now conspicuously absent.

> *Behold I tell you a mystery: we shall all indeed rise again.... The dead shall rise again incorruptible, and we shall be changed. For this corruptible must put on incorruption, and this mortal, must put on immortality. And when this mortal hath put on immortality, then shall come to pass the saying that is written: Death is swallowed up in victory. O death, where is thy victory? O death where is thy sting?...But thanks be to God, Who hath given us the victory through our Lord Jesus Christ. (1 Cor 15:51–57)*

Father Duffo readily recalled the words of the New Orleans *Daily Picayune* the month before: "[They are] fallen at their posts, dead in the arms of victory. No earthly warfare did they wage, for the spoils are Heaven."[389]

At the end of the solemn Mass, Father Duffo removed his chasuble and vested himself with a black cope and, in a brief but emotional ritual, sprinkled holy water on the graves of Father Pierre and Father Le Vézouët and then the catafalque. It was as if he was also blessing the many new graves—including the mass grave containing over eight hundred in the City Cemetery. He incensed both graves and then the catafalque. In the church shone together the elements of the late epidemic, but all made holy and fragrant: the water, the fire and the smoke.

All Honor to the Noble Martyrs

All honor to the noble martyrs and shame to those who cannot remember so noble a sacrifice and the fulfillment of so sublime and unselfish discharge of duty.
—Daily Shreveport Times, *November 23, 1883*

Cathedral of the Immaculate Conception, Natchitoches, Louisiana
Monday, November 3, 1873
All Souls' Day

As Father Duffo celebrated Mass in Shreveport, so did Bishop Martin in the cathedral in Natchitoches. Of all days, the Commemoration of All the Faithful Departed focused the heart on contemplation of the afterlife. While the life expectancy of New World missionary priests had been grim for centuries, on this day, there was even more to bear. Five saintly and selfless Christian martyrs were gone: among the faithful departed commemorated. Bishop Martin sought to record their heroics, to celebrate their "good" deaths and lament the loss of their talents and their friendship.

Bishop Martin now wrote a very different kind of letter than that of just two months before, when he pleaded for Father Louis Gergaud to return to Monroe. Yet his thoughts on both occasions were full of reminiscences about the fervor of the young missionary priests he recruited from Brittany.

Across twenty years as bishop of a diocese reliant on missionaries, Bishop Martin became quite accustomed to writing the Society for the Propagation of the Faith in Paris to report on activities of the new diocese. With joy he often wrote about steady growth—from five clergymen, seven churches, one religious order and one school when he was ordained in November 1853 to twenty-nine clergy, twenty-six churches and chapels, eight religious orders and seventeen schools by 1873.

This report was entirely different. This was to be a letter of "the losses and the sorrows." "Inscrutable, truly, are the ways of the Lord. I adore them and I accept them with my whole soul," he wrote to the Society in Paris, mourning "the irreparable losses" to his diocese and his own personal pain caused by the epidemic.

> *Gentlemen:*
>
> *You may have learned from the Paris newspapers that a pestilential fever, with a deadliness heretofore unknown in Louisiana, broke out about the end of August in Shreveport, a commercial city of ten thousand, in the extreme northwest of my diocese. There it caused and continues to cause dreadful ravages, the extent of which we will not know until later. That which the newspapers could not tell you, gentlemen, is of the irreparable losses to my diocese and my pain as bishop, in seeing fall, in the space of three weeks, five of my priests and among them, the three most eminent members of my clergy. In a rare assemblage of priestly virtues, of science and of talents, three had joined the Mission in 1854 and had reached maturity while producing an apostolic career filled with work and rich in the fruits of life which will live after them.*

The lengthy narrative considered the personal sacrifice of each "martyr to his charity." He wrote of them in the order of their deaths and penned the equivalent of a eulogy. He memorialized each priest with a mix of prose that included a practical recounting of their ministries, praise for their virtues and even offered glimpses into their personalities. They had labored together; they were his friends.

> *The first victim chosen by God was Mr. Isidore Quémerais, age 26, from the Diocese of Rennes, vicar in Shreveport. Mr. Father Quémerais was one of the seven young Bretons who followed me to Louisiana on my return from the Vatican Council. The piety, the gentleness, the unselfish dedication of*

this young priest, his filial affection for his bishop and the ease with which he mastered the difficulties of the English language permitted me to place great hope in him for the future. This was a flower; the angels gathered him for heaven. After two years of his ministry and while practicing the charity that immolates, he died on September 15th.

The next day marked the death of one of the most saintly priests that I have known in my long career: Mr. Father Pierre, founder of the missions in Bayou Pierre, Minden and Shreveport, whom you will learn more about from the account of his life and work, published in the Catholic Propagator, *which I have the honor of sending you. Long since, his excellent reputation had reached past the limits of my humble diocese and to keep such a treasure, it was necessary, more than once, to defend him against the truly justified esteem of several of my venerable colleagues, who saw in him a worthy candidate for the episcopate. The good Lord had given us this treasure; he has taken him away: may his Holy Name be blessed.*

On the 26th Mr. Father Biler died. He was chaplain of the novitiate and boarding school of the Daughters of the Cross at Fairfield. This excellent priest, 33 years old, from Diocese of Saint-Brieuc et Tréguier, had been in our mission only two and a half years. He had given up everything in Brittany, through the entreaties of Rev. Mother Le Conniat, his relative, to dedicate himself to this establishment to which it was impossible for me to provide a priest. At the first news of the illness of his confreres, he went to them, appointed himself their guardian, assisted them in their last moments and blessed their tombs. Left alone at the height of the plague, he called upon the charity of Messrs. Father Gergaud and Father Le Vézouët. The first arrived only a few days later to see him fall in his turn and to provide him with the consolations which he had given to the others at the expense of his own precious life.

Mr. Father Gergaud, from the Diocese of Nantes, ordained a priest for the diocese of Natchitoches in 1854, founder and pastor of the mission of Monroe for eighteen years, Vicar Forane, appointed by the bishop, for all of the districts situated between the Mississippi and the Red River valley, was a true "Homo Dei." Endowed with a very energetic nature, an elevated and cultivated spirit, patient and ardent zeal, a tender and generous heart protected by a prudent and reserved manner, Mr. Father Gergaud was a torch spreading light and heat around him. In a place where never before had a priest resided, where I had nothing to offer him but the unfinished skeleton of a chapel and a few diffident Christians, and where I doubted that he could live, Mr. Father Gergaud founded and leaves behind him a flourishing mission: church, presbytery, convent, Catholic school for boys, a large cemetery for the exclusive use of the faithful—he created it all; and in a period of eighteen years, his expenses for the honor of the religion exceeded two hundred thousand francs, of which I had allocated him barely ten thousand from the society. It is because his faith, while giving him the courage for any undertaking, also gave him the power to open the hearts and instill some of the generosity of his own soul. Through his outstanding talents, his priestly virtues and his work, Mr. Father Gergaud was a veritable power in Monroe: and because of his incontestable superiority, he was the leader of the diocesan clergy. At the time of the last Provincial Council, to which he accompanied me as a theologian, I nominated him to my venerable colleagues and he was readily accepted as my successor to the see of Natchitoches. Such a great consolation was to be denied me.

Upon receiving Mr. Father Biler's letter calling him to his aid, Mr. Father Gergaud left without a moment's hesitation. His only directive to his assistant, Mr. Quelard, was: "Write to Monseigneur at once; tell him that I am going to my death, that it is my duty and that I am leaving." He lived only ten days in Shreveport. Welcomed by all as a Godsent angel, he over-extended himself during one week to satisfy all the needs; he exerted himself beyond measure. There were more than one thousand sick people, of that number, perhaps fewer than twenty-five were Catholic but, in the presence of death, it was the priest that everyone called for; and God alone knows how many souls owe their salvation to the heroism of the Catholic priest. Meanwhile, Mr. Father Biler was stricken; he died on the 27th, assisted by Mr. Father Gergaud. The following day Mr. Father Gergaud was also mortally stricken and he died on October 1st, consoled and purified by the ministrations of one of his holiest and best-loved confreres, Mr. Father Le Vézouët, who, like the others, was a victim destined for death.

Mr. Father Le Vézouët, from a very Christian family of wealthy farmers of the Diocese of Saint-Brieuc et Tréguier, was endowed with a wide-ranging intelligence and a keen imagination. He had completed a brilliant course of classical and scientific studies and passed, with distinction, the examinations then required by the university for almost all of the liberal arts. Among all the careers open to him, he chose the serious and dedicated life of the priesthood and had completed his theological studies when, in 1854, he asked to follow me. After eighteen months of strengthening himself in his studies and in learning English, which he mastered easily, his talent for drawing young people to himself and his remarkable aptitude for teaching made me decide to entrust to him very particularly, the religious instruction and spiritual direction of St. Joseph College which I was establishing at Natchitoches in 1856 and in which, at the same time, he was teaching several classes. Shortly after, the president having retired, he succeeded him and with great zeal and success he directed, until 1862, the establishment which in that disastrous time, was completely devastated and ruined by the successive invasions of two belligerent armies. Hardly had he been relieved of the direction and his teaching at the college, when I entrusted him with the evangelization of the poor and degraded Mexicans, spread out between the Red River and the Sabine, whose language he spoke with ease. Although he usually resided in Natchitoches, where his presence had become indispensable to me, he regularly fulfilled this difficult Mission with the dedicated zeal that he brought to everything that he undertook; he did this as an apostle for nine years, instructing the people, validating marriages, building and furnishing churches and by the Divine Word and the grace of the sacraments, he elevated these unrefined people to the dignity of Christians. Finally, as his crowning achievement in this work, in 1871 he founded a permanent mission in Many, at the very center of this population. There he constructed a church with its presbytery, its cemetery, the lands necessary for the residence of a priest and he even installed, in the same year, a young confrere, successor of his zeal. Here Mr. Father Le Vézouët was one of the three members of the episcopal council, diocesan director and zealous promoter of the works of the Propagation of the Faith and the Holy Childhood, chaplain of the convent of the Sisters of Mercy and director of a day school which he founded for boys; responsible, moreover, for several small missions at a short distance from Natchitoches, for preaching in English at the Cathedral and for a large number of penitents. But, above all, Mr. Father Le Vézouët was the friend, the consoler, the priest of the children, of the afflicted, and of the poor. Whatever time these rigid demands left to him, he used for them, he spent with them; going from cabin to cabin, bringing encouragement, consolation and alms to all.

On September 19th, Mr. Father Le Vézouët returned to Natchitoches after an eight day mission on the left bank of the Red River. After having told him of Mr. Father Biler's request to me that he be sent immediately to Shreveport, I asked him, "What would you like to do, my son?" He replied, "Monseigneur, if you tell me to leave, I leave; if you leave it up to me, I stay." He realized that I was searching his eyes for the real meaning of his response, and he added: "I want to go so much that if you left the decision up to me, I would believe that in going, I was acting according to my own will and I do not want to do anything but the will of God." "If it is so," I replied to him, "go." He spent one more day to put his affairs in order and to visit several families for the last time. The news of his imminent departure spread quickly and to those who said, "You are going to your death," he replied: "I believe it, but I know that I am taking the surest and the shortest path to heaven." Because other means of transportation were lacking, Mr. Father Le Vézouët had to undertake the 110 mile journey to Shreveport on horseback. He arrived there to find Mr. Father Gergaud mortally ill and gave him the assistance and consolations of the Holy Church. Shortly after, he began to sink under the inexorable attacks of the plague. He had foreseen this and had telegraphed the Archbishop of New Orleans, requesting two priests. A Jesuit father and an assistant from the cathedral left on October 3rd; they arrived soon enough to console him in his last moments and to open heaven to him. He died on the 8th, having completed his fortieth year in the eighteenth year of his priesthood.

Gentlemen, I have often spoken to you of the growing prosperity of my mission and its hopes for the future. Today I have told you of the losses and the sorrows. The hand of God has struck me and with these priests, pride of the priesthood, the crown of my old age has fallen. Inscrutable, truly, are the ways of the Lord. I adore them and I accept them with my whole soul, and I can only say: Happy is the diocese that could lose such men, happy is the earth watered by their sweat and sanctified by their death. Martyrs to charity or martyrs to persecution, in their venerated tombs will grow the deepest roots of the Holy Church of the One whose death was our life.

Pray, gentlemen, that before my own death, I may find worthy successors to the ministry and the admirable virtues of these saintly priests.

Aug. Marie Martin, Bishop of Natchitoches

For some time after the death of Father Gergaud, the communities of Shreveport and Monroe disputed over custody of his mortal remains. Catholics in Monroe organized a formal memorial association, and within days of his death, parishioners met and passed a resolution calling for his exhumation and reburial at St. Matthew's.

> *Be it resolved, by the Catholics of Ouachita Parish, that the death of Father Louis Gergaud, parish priest of St. Matthew's Church…where he has been a zealous worker in the cause of the Holy Catholic Church for the last eighteen years….Be it resolved further, that as soon as circumstances*

Grave of Father Louis Gergaud, St. Matthew's Cemetery, Monroe, Louisiana. *Authors' collection.*

> *permit, we will have his remains brought to this city and interred, according to his last wish, in the Catholic cemetery in this place…and erect a suitable monument to his memory.*[390]

Aware of the wishes of Monroe Catholics, the organized Catholics of Shreveport passed a competing but similar resolution on November 30, 1873:

> *Resolved, that whereas the Catholics of Ouachita Parish passed a resolution at their meeting held in Monroe on the 4th of October, to remove to Monroe the remains of their late pastor Father Louis Gergaud, and whereas we feel we also have a claim to his ashes, as it was in our cause and amongst us and for us that he died.*[391]

In late January 1874, the successor of Father Gergaud came to Shreveport to reclaim his remains and return them to Monroe.[392] Father Enaut accompanied the body to Monroe, arriving on February 3, and there was a solemn gathering in St. Matthew's until his re-interment in the church cemetery on February 4.[393]

†

After the heroic martyrdom of the first five, two priests remained in the church militant. Father Charles S.M. Férec recovered completely, only to drown in Lake Pontchartrain in New Orleans less than two years later. Father James J. Duffo served as the interim parish priest in Shreveport until his permanent replacement could arrive. Bishop Martin assigned Father Joseph Gentille to Shreveport and its stations in Minden, Keachi, Les Presles and Bellevue. The new pastor had been a close friend of the late Father Gergaud, ordained in the same Diocese of Nantes. He became pastor of Holy Trinity on All Hallowed's Eve, near the end of the epidemic,[394] but Fathers Duffo and Férec did not depart Shreveport until December 10. Interestingly, Father Duffo returned to Shreveport after Christmas, performing a wedding on December 29, no doubt a reflection of friendships made during his ministry in the epidemic.[395]

Bishop Martin took an active interest in the fate of the Shreveport orphans and worked closely with Father Duffo to find shelter and care for them.[396] Ultimately, the idea of funding a permanent orphanage never gained traction following Father Duffo's return to New Orleans.[397] The children were scattered across the region to various Catholic boardinghouses with open beds; this was the best the Church could then muster.

Beginning November 6, the Howard Association ceased raising funds, as it was projected the reserves would hold out until the city had recovered.[398] While the Howards had begun to demobilize, some of the public health improvement ideas born of the epidemic began to take root. Chief among them was the establishment of a permanent public charity hospital in Shreveport, which opened its doors to the city in 1876.

Meanwhile, the memory of five priests who gave their lives in 1873 Shreveport was burned into the community story until the present day. People witnessed the free offering of their lives and remembered. Their service to strangers of the stricken city was without comparison, and the people of Shreveport knew it.

As Bishop Martin was writing the letter to the Propagation of the Faith, his own death was but twenty-three months away; his decline in health might be measured in proportion to the grief of his emotional loss. Indeed, his future official correspondence at times continued to give heartrending insights into his ongoing grief. For example, he poignantly reflected on Father Le Vézouët in a January 1874 letter to the Society for the Propagation of the Faith, as he lamented the challenges of replacing so worthy a priest:

Memorial stained-glass windows at Holy Trinity Church in Shreveport. *Authors' collection.*

He was a zealous diocesan director of this work…and as you know, dear sirs, this saintly priest is dead, on the 8th day of October, a voluntary victim of his devotion for the plague victims of Shreveport, and he had left Natchitoches at the end of September, leaving nothing but some notes, enough for him, but not enough for others.[399]

Detail of the memorial stained-glass window at Holy Trinity Church in Shreveport. *Authors' collection.*

On September 29, 1875, Bishop Auguste Marie Martin died in Natchitoches. With the considerable accomplishment of shepherding a fledgling diocese into full bloom and having himself been both missionary and emissary, he joined his Breton recruits and confreres in eternal life. Even in the midst of so much death, the eternal rhythm of the life of the Church marched on with its divinely appointed order.

†

On February 3, 1876, a lengthy procession formed before Holy Trinity Church, despite it being a busy Thursday morning. Business would wait on this day. With a cross-bearer leading them, the group of parishioners, joined by other citizens, walked toward City Cemetery six blocks away to collect the mortal remains of their first vicar, Father Isidore Quémerais. He was to also rest under the sanctuary of the church, next to Father Pierre and Father Le Vézouët.

Father Joseph Gentille leading, the coffin containing the body of Father Isidore Quémerais was reverently placed on a bier. Along the way back to the church, the people of Shreveport paused on downtown streets, moved by the public procession and pausing to remember the reason for it. Then, a solemn Mass of Requiem was offered, sung by the students of St. Vincent's

Academy. Officiating was Reverend Father Joseph Aubree of Many, Louisiana; Reverend Father Tom Laughery of Marshall, Texas, acting deacon; and Reverend Father V. Pellonin of Shreveport, sub-deacon, with Reverend Father Hennessy of Jefferson, Texas, orator of the day.[400] With every appropriate honor given him, Father Quémerais was placed below the high altar, next to his pastor. Eight years later, the remains of the three priests would be moved to the new Catholic cemetery in town.

The afternoon sun of March 1884 probably did little to warm the sanctuary when the men tore at the cold dirt and dust beneath the church with shovels. They removed the floorboards near the base of the altar and worked in a tight space. Father François Le Vézouët had been buried beneath Holy Trinity's altar for ten years, five months and four days, since October 9, 1873. The coffin was found badly decayed. Around one o'clock, "the precious bones" of the martyr to his charity were sufficiently recovered. His vestments were dust, but Father Le Vézouët's remains were identifiable by those who remembered him by his "luxuriant and beautiful black"[401] head of hair, which remained almost wholly intact. His remains were placed in a new coffin, the men noting as they did so that there was no offensive smell. The remains would await a worthy reburial, but the workmen were finished for the day.[402]

The next afternoon was again clear and cool. Under the watchful eye of Father Joseph Gentille, the work continued with the grave of Father Jean Pierre. It took great effort to lift the iron casket from the tomb, and as the coffin was freed from the earth, water was heard sloshing inside and was soon witnessed seeping from crevices. The four men strained to turn the casket head up. Water then rushed out and emptied back into the grave below. Satisfied with the condition of the martyr's coffin, Father Gentille waved off any offers to remove the remains for a new casket. Father Pierre was placed near Father Le Vézouët overnight.

At ten o'clock the following morning, the men gathered again to open the grave containing Father Isidore Quémerais. His wooden coffin, found decaying but somewhat intact, was removed with equal reverence. The men transferred his remains to a new coffin. The women of the Ladies Altar Society of Holy Trinity gathered and spent the day lavishly decorating the church for another greatly anticipated High Requiem Mass.[403]

†

Thunderstorms brought torrents of rain beginning around one thirty on the morning of Saturday, March 22. The streets were temporarily flooded and quickly turned to muck in the areas where there were yet no brick pavers installed. Then, at six o'clock, an early morning rainbow shone brightly—signaling an end to the showers that again threatened to delay the ceremonies. Father Gentille began Mass promptly at seven o'clock with the congregation crowded in the church. Two new wooden caskets flanked Father Pierre's cleaned but original iron sarcophagus.[404]

At ten o'clock, the cortege solemnly commenced with Father Gentille following four altar boys. The first carried Holy Trinity's processional cross, with the three behind him carrying crosses bound for each of the French missionaries' new tombs. The caskets of the yellow fever martyrs were conveyed behind the priests in attendance. Joining the procession were the sisters of St. Mary's Academy and of St. Vincent's, along with more than twenty carriages of laymen and women. This solemn procession covered more than two miles along the Texas Road through intermittent showers and reached the new Catholic cemetery gates at eleven o'clock, where three empty tombs awaited the reception of the martyred remains. Father Gentille was assisted by Father Napoleon Joseph Rolleaux, and the pair blessed each vault in succession. Father Gentille expressed the heartfelt thanks of the

The final resting place of Father Isidore Quémerais, Father Jean Pierre and Father Francois Le Vézouët at St. Joseph's Cemetery in Shreveport. *Authors' collection.*

people of Shreveport for their lives of selfless ministry. The caskets were gently lowered into their brick, stone and cement tombs. Then, through the length of another rain shower, the brickmasons went to work sealing the martyrs' basal tombs.[405]

> *Inscrutable, truly, are the ways of the Lord. I adore them and I accept them with my whole soul, and I can only say: Happy is the diocese that could lose such men, happy is the earth watered by their sweat and sanctified by their death. Martyrs to charity or martyrs to persecution, in their venerated tombs will grow the deepest roots of the Holy Church of the One whose death was our life.*[406]
>
> *Adieu, dear sons.* Custodiat vos Dominum semper*! May the Lord keep you always.*

NOTES

Introduction

1. Archdiocese of St. Louis, MO.
2. Correspondence of Archbishop Antoine Blanc, Archives of the Archdiocese of New Orleans, LA; Calendar of Letters, Archives of the University of Notre Dame, South Bend, IN.
3. Correspondence of Bishop Auguste Martin to the Society for the Propagation of the Faith, MPFP-096, Archives of the University of Notre Dame.
4. Ibid.
5. Ibid.
6. Diocese of St. Brieuc and Treguier, Archives.
7. D'Antoni, "Bayou Pierre: Land of Yesteryear."
8. Correspondence of Bishop Auguste Martin.
9. Annual Reports of Bishop Auguste Martin.
10. Ibid.
11. Correspondence of Bishop Auguste Martin.
12. Ibid.
13. *Morning Star and Catholic Messenger*, August 6, 1870.
14. Correspondence of Bishop Auguste Martin.

Prologue

15. Letter of Bishop Auguste Martin to Father Louis Gergaud, September 30, 1873, Daughters of the Cross Collection, Noel Archives and Special Collections, Louisiana State University at Shreveport.

The Surest Path to Heaven

16. Levee Street is known contemporaneously as Commerce Street.
17. *Daily Shreveport Times*, September 27–28, 1873; *Shreveport Journal*, June 17, 1935.
18. *Shreveport Journal*, June 17, 1935; *Daily Shreveport Times*, November 15, 1873; *Ouachita Telegraph*, October 3, 1873.
19. *Daily Shreveport Times*, September 28, 1873.
20. Correspondence of Mother Mary Hyacinth Le Conniat, Daughters of the Cross Collection, Noel Archives and Special Collections, Louisiana State University at Shreveport.
21. Luke 12:8.
22. *Daily Shreveport Times*, September 21, 1873; September 30, 1873.
23. Correspondence of Bishop Auguste Martin.
24. Ibid.
25. Ibid.
26. Ibid.
27. Ibid.
28. *Catholic Encyclopedia*. The name has nothing to do with embers or ashes. It is most likely a corruption of *quatuor tempora* through Dutch, Danish or German (*Quatember*). Ember Days remind the faithful of a time when society was mostly rural.
29. *Missale Romanum*.
30. Correspondence of Bishop Auguste Martin.
31. Ibid. The LeVézouët family played a prominent role in rebuilding a modern church on the original medieval site.
32. Ignatius, *Across Three Centuries*, 195.
33. Correspondence of Mother Mary Hyacinth Le Conniat.
34. Ibid.
35. Ibid; correspondence of Bishop Auguste Martin.

At Every Corner

36. Howard Association, "Report of the Committee," 10; *Times-Picayune*, October 6, 1878.
37. *New Orleans Times*, October 15, 1875; *Times-Picayune*, October 6, 1878; *New Orleans Price-Current, Commercial Intelligencer and Merchants' Transcript*, July 5, 1873.
38. Howard Association, "Report of the Committee," 10; *Times-Picayune*, October 6, 1878; *Republican*, June 27, 1873; July 12, 1873; *Boston Medical and Surgical Journal* 89, 544.
39. Woodworth, *Annual Report*, 102, 210; Booth, *Inaugural Dissertation*, 77; *Boston Medical and Surgical Journal* 90, 154; *Republican*, July 12, 1873; *Times-Picayune*, October 6, 1878. A chambermaid aboard the *C.H. Durfee* named Nancy would be among the first to perish in Shreveport. It is probable she contracted the illness while in New Orleans.
40. This was the description Rear Admiral David Dixon Porter gave to the Red River in official reports during the Union Red River Campaign in the Civil War.
41. Tyson, *Red River in Southwestern History*, 94.
42. Conveyance Record Book 24, Natchitoches Parish Courthouse, 68.
43. O'Pry, *Chronicles of Shreveport*, 322.
44. Tyson, *Red River in Southwestern History*, 94–95.
45. Colonial Dames, *Historical Profile of Shreveport*, 3.
46. *New Orleans Weekly Picayune*, as cited in Colonial Dames, *Historical Profile of Shreveport*, 5–6.
47. Colonial Dames, *Historical Profile of Shreveport*, 5–6.
48. United States Census, 1860.
49. United States Census, 1860.
50. Howard Association, "Report of the Committee," 12.
51. Booth, *Inaugural Dissertation*, 3–4; *Boston Medical and Surgical Journal* 90, 73; Howard Association, "Report of the Committee," 6.
52. Booth, *Inaugural Dissertation*, 6–7.
53. Ibid.
54. Woodworth, *Annual Report*, 1873, 110; Johnson, "Great Yellow Fever Epidemic," 97.
55. *Boston Medical and Surgical Journal* 90, 73.
56. Booth, *Inaugural Dissertation*, 3. "The withering hand of political adventurers." This situation is even captured in a panoramic photograph of the city taken from the Red River, with rubbish and driftwood seen in piles throughout the commercial district.

57. Currie's Spring was located just south of the downtown central business district, named for Andrew Currie, a parishioner of Holy Trinity Church and a future mayor of Shreveport.
58. One of the best surviving examples of such a cistern is located at 209 Texas Street, which in 1873 housed the medical office of Dr. Joseph Moore and Lewis Druggist, a heavily trafficked treatment location for yellow fever victims.

Much Sickness May Result

59. Johnson, "Great Yellow Fever Epidemic," 97.
60. *Daily Shreveport Times*, August 12, 1873.
61. Woodworth, *Annual Report*, 1873, 238; Transactions of the Medical Association of the State of Alabama: 27th Session, 1874, 123; *Daily Shreveport Times*, August 13, 1873.
62. Woodworth, *Annual Report*, 1873, 238.
63. Ibid.; transactions of the Medical Association of the State of Alabama, 124, 126.
64. *Daily Shreveport Times*, August 20, 1873.
65. Woodworth, *Annual Report*, 1873, 110; Woodworth, *Annual Report*, 1874, 238; *Daily Shreveport Times*, August 20, 1873; *Biographical and Historical Memoirs of Northwest Louisiana*, 47.
66. Major yellow fever outbreaks occurred in Shreveport in 1837, 1845 and 1853.
67. *Daily Shreveport Times*, August 21, 1873; August 22, 1873.
68. Woodworth, *Annual Report*, 1874, 238.
69. Sacred Heart Catholic Church, Moreauville, Louisiana, www.shcmoreauville.org.
70. Ron Downing, "The Rev. Louis Gergaud Established First Parochial School in Monroe Over 150 Years Ago," *Ouachita Citizen*, September 14, 2016.
71. Luke 12:35–44.
72. Booth, *Inaugural Dissertation*, 10–11. Sources disagree here, with some suggesting the men were actually treated and discharged. In either case, medical help failed to save them.
73. Booth, *Inaugural Dissertation*. Some contemporaneous sources suggest the men were turned away without treatment because they were from out of town, but it seems likely they simply did not have the ability to pay.

It is known from the advertisements of the Market Street Infirmary that services cost five dollars per day.

74. *Daily Shreveport Times*, August 21, 1873.
75. Howard Association, "Report of the Committee," 9; Booth, *Inaugural Dissertation*, 10–11.
76. Woodworth, *Annual Report*, 1874, 239; *Daily Shreveport Times*, August 23, 1873.
77. According to reports in the *Daily Shreveport Times*, among the steamers plying the waters in front of the city were the *R.T. Bryerly*, the *Royal George*, the *Theodore W. Sterling*, the *Clifford* and the *Carrie E. Thorn*.
78. *Daily Shreveport Times*, August 24, 1873.
79. Ibid.
80. Joiner and White, *Shreveport's Oakland Cemetery*, 81. Lieutenant Woodruff was a West Point graduate and a Civil War veteran—an officer serving the Union as the war came to a violent close. A native of Iowa, he first came to Shreveport in 1871. Lieutenant Woodruff was a talented engineer, surveyor, photographer and demonstrated leader of men.
81. *Daily Shreveport Times*, August 31, 1873. In 1872, Shreveport agents recorded the arrival of 375 steamers to the river port, responsible for offloading more than eighty-two thousand tons of cargo and taking back to their home ports countless cotton bales and head of cattle.
82. O'Pry, *Chronicles of Shreveport*, 322.
83. "Report of the Committee on the Yellow Fever Epidemic," 7–8. In one Shreveport boardinghouse, located on Travis Street, twenty-two people perished from yellow fever during the epidemic (*Daily Shreveport Times*, November 15, 1873).
84. Luke 6:12–19.
85. *Daily Shreveport Times*, August 24, 1873.
86. Alabama Medical Association, *Transactions of the Medical Association*, 124–25; "Report of the Committee on the Yellow Fever Epidemic," 7–8.
87. *Daily Shreveport Times*, August 28, 1873.
88. Ibid.
89. Howard Association, "Report of the Committee," 11–12.
90. *Boston Medical and Surgical Journal* 90, 153; *Daily Shreveport Times*, August 30, 1873.
91. *Daily Shreveport Times*, August 30, 1873.
92. Sacramental Register of Holy Trinity Church, Shreveport, Louisiana.
93. Ibid.
94. The Roman Ritual contains all the prayers needed for priests outside the context of Mass.

Implore God to Have Pity

95. *Daily Shreveport Times*, September 2, 1873; *New Orleans Medical and Surgical Journal* 13, 169; *Boston Medical and Surgical Journal* 90, 74.
96. Booth, *Inaugural Dissertation*, 12.
97. *Daily Shreveport Times*, August 25, 1873; September 2, 1873.
98. Ibid., November 15, 1873.
99. Baer's body was returned somewhat unceremoniously for burial in the Hebrew Rest portion of the City Cemetery (renamed Oakland Cemetery in 1905).
100. *Daily Shreveport Times*, September 2, 1873.
101. *American Church Almanac and Yearbook: 1898–99*, 404; O'Pry, *Chronicles of Shreveport*, 220; Brock, *Shreveport Chronicles*, 72.
102. According to popular hagiography, this is believed to be Saint Lupus of Troyes, a fourth-century bishop, for whom an early popular devotion developed throughout France.
103. The Memorial of St. Blaise is celebrated on February 3. The formula for the blessing remains largely unchanged across the centuries.
104. Sebaste in historical Armenia (modern Sivas, Turkey).
105. Butler, *Lives of the Saints*, 301.
106. The Greek word *martyr* literally means "witness."
107. Records of the Grand Seminary of St. Brieuc-Treguier, Archives of the Diocese of St. Brieuc, France.
108. Ibid.
109. Matthew 19:27–29.
110. Sacramental Register of Holy Trinity Church. Verbiage in the marriage register for that entry, handwritten by Father Jean Pierre.
111. Correspondence of Bishop Auguste Martin.
112. Ibid.
113. Original photograph, Archives of the Diocese of Alexandria, Louisiana. An original *carte de visite* captured the likeness of Father Pierre and a boy. It is a poignant image, and on the reverse is written in script, "Father Pierre [and the] boy he was going to take care of him [*sic*]."
114. Register of the Daughters of the Cross.
115. *Daily Shreveport Times*, November 15, 1873.
116. Ibid.
117. Father Joseph Gentille, Pastor of Holy Trinity Church, Personal Diary, Archives of the Diocese of Shreveport, Louisiana.

118. Correspondence of Mother Mary Hyacinth Le Conniat; correspondence of Bishop Auguste Martin.
119. *Daily Shreveport Times*, November 15, 1873.
120. Crosby, *American Plague*, 56.
121. *Daily Shreveport Times*, September 2, 1873.
122. Today, "City Cemetery" is known as Oakland Cemetery.
123. *Daily Shreveport Times*, September 3, 1873.
124. Ibid.
125. Ibid.
126. Ibid., September 4, 1873.
127. Ibid.
128. Ibid., November 15, 1873.
129. Ibid., September 4, 1873; United States Census, 1870. The Howards used a modified version of the police jury city wards to organize their relief efforts. The Howard Association's Ward 1 does not appear to completely align with the U.S. Census Bureau's Ward 1. Ward 1 was the least populated in the 1870 census, while the opposite is likely true with the ward determined by the Howards. Joiner, PhD, personal interview, January 6, 2018.
130. *Daily Shreveport Times*, September 4, 1873.
131. Ibid., November 15, 1873.
132. Ibid.
133. Ibid., September 4, 1873.
134. Ibid., September 6, 1873.
135. Ibid., September 5, 1873.
136. Ibid.
137. Ibid.
138. Quoted in D'Antoni, Calendar of Letters, Archives of the University of Notre Dame, South Bend, IN.
139. *Daily Shreveport Times*, September 5, 1873; September 6, 1873.
140. *Shreveport Journal*, June 27, 1935.
141. *New York Times*, October 15, 1873
142. Matthew 6:24–33.
143. Prayer based on Luke 4:38–44 and the Collect of *Missa in Tempore Mortalitatis*.
144. *Daily Shreveport Times*, September 9, 1873.
145. Ibid.; September 10, 1873; *Jefferson Democrat*, September 13, 1873, as cited in Johnson, "Great Yellow Fever Epidemic," 98–99.

Blotted Out of Existence

146. *Daily Shreveport Times*, September 9, 1873; September 10, 1873.
147. Ibid., November 15, 1873; Sacramental Register of Holy Trinity Church.
148. *Daily Shreveport Times*, September 9, 1873; September 10, 1873; November 15, 1873.
149. McCants, *They Came to Louisiana*, 223.
150. *Daily Shreveport Times*, November 15, 1873.
151. Ibid., September 10, 1873.
152. Correspondence of Mother Mary Hyacinth Le Conniat; Records of Holy Trinity Church.
153. Elford, "Brief History of St. Vincent's Academy."
154. Ibid.
155. *Daily Shreveport Times*, November 15, 1873.
156. Ibid., September 11, 1873; November 15, 1873.
157. *Shreveport Journal*, June 27, 1935.
158. Letter of Lieutenant Eugene A. Woodruff, September 9, 1873, Noel Archives and Special Collections, Louisiana State University at Shreveport, Shreveport, Louisiana.
159. Ibid.
160. Correspondence of Mother Mary Hyacinth Le Conniat; Register of the Daughters of the Cross.
161. Correspondence of Mother Mary Hyacinth Le Conniat.
162. Correspondence of Bishop Auguste Martin; correspondence of Mother Mary Hyacinth Le Conniat.
163. Register of the Daughters of the Cross.
164. Ibid.
165. *Daily Shreveport Times*, September 11, 1873; November 15, 1873.
166. Ibid., September 13, 1873.
167. *New York Times*, September 30, 1873.
168. *Daily Shreveport Times*, September 13, 1873.
169. Hall, personal diary.
170. *Daily Shreveport Times*, November 15, 1873.
171. Ibid., September 11, 1873; September 13, 1873.
172. Steamers such as *C.H. Durfee*, *Flirt* and *Royal George*.
173. *Daily Shreveport Times*, September 12, 1873; September 13, 1873.
174. Ibid., September 12, 1873; September 13, 1873.
175. Ibid., September 20, 1873.

176. Ibid., September 13, 1873. Contemporary sources disagree whether the circus had spent any time in Mexico. However, most sources examined for this work suggest the circus never did.
177. Slout, *En Route to the Great Eastern Circus*, 108. It is clear Dingess was mistaken in his belief that he disembarked on the last steamer shortly after his arrival, but certainly that should have been true if the city had enforced the quarantine.
178. Drs. John J. Reilly and James F. Finney (who oversaw the clinical operations at the Howard's opera house–based hospital) and Henry Smith.
179. *New York Times*, September 15, 1873.
180. Correspondence of Mother Mary Hyacinth Le Conniat.
181. Ibid.
182. Ibid.

One Great Charnel House

183. *Daily Shreveport Times*, September 13, 1873.
184. Daughters of the Cross, "Victims of 1873 Yellow Fever Epidemic."
185. *Daily Shreveport Times*, September 13, 1873.
186. As later quoted in *Shreveport Journal*, June 27, 1935.
187. *Daily Shreveport Times*, September 13, 1873.
188. Horace, as quoted by Saint Alphonsus de Liguori.
189. Correspondence of Mother Mary Hyacinth Le Conniat.
190. Ibid.
191. Ibid.
192. Scudder, *Eclectic Medical Journal*, vol. 34.
193. Ibid.
194. Hall, personal diary, September 14, 1873.
195. *Daily Shreveport Times*, September 17, 1873.
196. Correspondence of Bishop Auguste Martin.
197. *Roman Missal.*
198. Etymology of excruciating: *ex* = from and *cruce* = cross. A pain that is excruciating is as if it were experienced from the cross.
199. "Have among yourselves the same attitude that is also yours in Christ Jesus, Who, though he was in the form of God, did not regard equality with God something to be grasped. Rather, he emptied himself, taking the form of a slave, coming in human likeness; and found human in appearance, he humbled himself, becoming obedient to death, even death

on a cross. Because of this, God greatly exalted him and bestowed on him the name that is above every name, that at the name of Jesus every knee should bend, of those in heaven and on earth and under the earth, and every tongue confess that Jesus Christ is Lord, to the glory of God the Father. Philippians 2:5–11

200. "By the sign of the holy cross, O Lord, protect Your people from the deceits of their every foe, that our service may be pleasing to You and our offering acceptable, alleluia!" Offertory Antiphon.
201. The Secret of the Mass.
202. The Post-Communion Prayer of the Mass.
203. Correspondence of Mother Mary Hyacinth Le Conniat.
204. Ibid.
205. Ibid.
206. Ibid.
207. *Daily Shreveport Times*, September 17, 1873.
208. Scudder, *Eclectic Medical Journal.*
209. Ibid.
210. Correspondence of Mother Mary Hyacinth Le Conniat.
211. Ibid.
212. Ibid.

The Busy Carnival of Misery

213. *Daily Shreveport Times*, September 15, 1873.
214. Ibid., September 17, 1873.
215. Johnson, "Great Yellow Fever Epidemic," 99; *Shreveport Journal*, June 27, 1935.
216. Records of Holy Trinity Church, Archives of the Diocese of Shreveport, Louisiana.
217. Correspondence of Mother Mary Hyacinth Le Conniat.
218. Ibid.
219. Ibid.
220. Ibid.
221. *Nashville Union and American*, September 17, 1873; *New Orleans Republican*, September 17, 1873; *Times-Picayune*, September 17, 1873.
222. Register of the Daughters of the Cross.
223. Ibid.

224. Correspondence of Mother Mary Hyacinth Le Conniat.
225. Daughters of the Cross, "Victims of 1873 Yellow Fever Epidemic."
226. Antiphon for the invitatory.
227. Correspondence of Mother Mary Hyacinth Le Conniat.
228. *Journal of the Telegraph*, November 15, 1873; Baudier Historical Collection.
229. Baudier Historical Collection.
230. *Daily Shreveport Times*, September 17, 1873.
231. Correspondence of Bishop Auguste Martin.
232. *Daily Shreveport Times*, November 15, 1873.
233. Correspondence of Bishop Auguste Martin.
234. *Daily Shreveport Times*, September 17, 1873.
235. Ibid., September 18, 1873.

I Go to My Death

236. Hall, personal diary, September 18–19, 1873.
237. Ibid.
238. $100.00 in 1873 is equivalent to $2,264.91 in 2020.
239. *Daily Shreveport Times*, September 18, 1873; September 19, 1873. September 20, 1873; *New York Times*, September 26, 1873.
240. *Daily Shreveport Times*, September 18, 1873; Johnson, "Great Yellow Fever Epidemic," 101–2.
241. *Daily Shreveport Times*, September 18, 1873; *Frank Leslie's Illustrated Newspaper*, October 4, 1873.
242. *Daily Shreveport Times*, September 19, 1873.
243. Ibid., September 20, 1873.
244. Baudier Historical Collection.
245. Ibid.
246. Ibid.
247. Correspondence of Bishop Auguste Martin.
248. Ibid.
249. Annual Reports of Bishop Auguste Martin; correspondence of Bishop Auguste Martin.
250. Correspondence of Father Louis Gergaud to Bishop Antoine Jaquemet of Nantes, Archives of the Diocese of Nantes, France.
251. This is a reference to Father Jean Baptiste Avenard, priest of the Diocese of Natchitoches, whom Bishop Martin also recruited from Brittany for the Louisiana missions.

252. The reference to Father Claver is to St. Peter Claver, who was a seventeenth-century Jesuit missionary among the slaves of the colonial New World. At the time of Father Gergaud's writing of this letter, Claver had only recently been beatified in 1850.
253. Correspondence of Father Louis Gergaud.
254. Ibid.
255. Baudier Historical Collection.
256. Ibid.
257. Ibid.
258. Ouachita Parish History, unpublished manuscript, Archives of St. Matthew's Church, Monroe, Louisiana.
259. Ibid.
260. Martin, "Notice on Very Rev. Father Gergaud."
261. Ibid.
262. Correspondence of Mother Mary Hyacinth Le Conniat.
263. *Daily Shreveport Times*, November 15, 1873.
264. Ibid.
265. Ibid., September 20, 1873.
266. Ibid., September 21, 1873.

In Another World

267. Louis Gergaud birth record, Vital Records of Héric, France, copy of original in possession of the authors. Louis Gergaud was born on March 22, 1832, to parents Sébastian and Anne Father Gergaud.
268. Sacramental Register of St. Nicholas Church, Héric, France.
269. Records of the Grand Seminary of Nantes, Archives of the Diocese of Nantes, France.
270. Ibid.
271. Ordination Records of the Diocese of Nantes, Archives of the Diocese of Nantes, France.
272. Correspondence of Father Louis Gergaud.
273. Correspondence of Mother Mary Hyacinth Le Conniat.
274. Scudder, *Eclectic Medical Journal*, 145–46; *New Orleans Medical and Surgical Journal*, 30. Cathartics, such as Oleum Ricini, Magnesia, doses of calomel, quinine or pulverized ipecac, were common. We know from contemporary accounts that supplies of ice were made available at the railroad depot at least during the month of September.

275. Correspondence of Mother Mary Hyacinth Le Conniat,
276. Ibid.
277. *Daily Shreveport Times*, September 23, 1873. Schurr's date of death: Sunday, September 21, 1873.
278. *Daily Shreveport Times*, September 27, 1873
279. Ibid.; *New York Times*, September 23, 1873.
280. Correspondence of James Muse Dabbs, Ouachita County (Parish) Louisiana Archives History, accessed at www.usgwarchives.net; *New York Times*, September 23, 1873; Baudier Historical Collection.
281. Correspondence of Bishop Auguste Martin.
282. Correspondence of James Muse Dabbs.
283. *Rapides Gazette*, October 25, 1873.
284. Hall, personal diary, September 22–23, 1873.
285. Ibid.
286. Scudder, *Eclectic Medical Journal*, 144.
287. Hall, personal diary, September 22–23, 1873.
288. Ibid., September 26, 1873.
289. *Daily Shreveport Times*, September 26, 1873; *New York Times*, September 23, 1873.
290. *Daily Shreveport Times*, September 26, 1873.
291. Ibid.; September 27, 1873; *New York Times*, September 30, 1873; *Louisiana Democrat*, October 1, 1873. See also Miciotto, "Shreveport's First Major Health Crisis" and O'Pry, *Chronicles of Shreveport*, 1928.
292. *Daily Shreveport Times*, September 23, 1873; September 24, 1873.
293. Ibid., September 24, 1873.
294. Ibid., September 25, 1873; September 27, 1873.
295. Ibid., September 25, 1873; September 27, 1873.
296. Correspondence of Mother Mary Hyacinth Le Conniat.
297. Ibid.
298. Ibid. Perhaps this statement indicates he was also confirming deathbed Christians.
299. Ibid.
300. Ibid.
301. Ibid.
302. Ibid.

A Tempest of Death

303. *Daily Shreveport Times*, October 1, 1873
304. Ibid.
305. United States Census, 1870.
306. *Daily Shreveport Times*, June 23, 1872; August 24, 1872.
307. Ibid., March 28, 1873.
308. Hale, Joiner, Palombo and White, *Wicked Shreveport*, 16; United States Census, 1870; *Daily Shreveport Times*, October 1, 1873.
309. Hale, Joiner, Palombo and White, *Wicked Shreveport*; *Daily Shreveport Times*, October 1, 1873. In a somewhat macabre footnote to an already bizarre tale, in 2008, an inspection was conducted by public authorities of human remains that surfaced from within the mass grave in Oakland Cemetery (formerly known as the City Cemetery) in the section commonly referred to as the yellow fever mound. The ghoulish find included his sternum and rib cage, with a discharged .32-caliber ball lodged in one of the bones.
310. *Daily Shreveport Times*, November 15, 1873.
311. *New York Times*, September 30, 1873; *The World*, September 30, 1873.
312. Sacramental Register of Holy Trinity Church, Shreveport, Louisiana.
313. Matthew 22:35–46.
314. Saturday, May 3, 1856, was the date of ordination of François Le Vézouët.
315. Father Louis Gergaud Diary, Archives of St. Matthew's Church, Monroe, Louisiana.
316. His final resting place would ultimately become the same cemetery he established in Monroe.
317. Letter of Bishop Auguste Martin to Father Louis Gergaud, September 30, 1873.
318. Reverend F.T. Rawson, "Memorial of Father Louis Gergaud," *Ouachita Telegraph*, October 24, 1873.
319. Grave marker inscription of Father Louis Gergaud, St. Matthew's Church cemetery, Monroe, Louisiana.
320. *Daily Shreveport Times*, October 2, 1873.
321. *New York Times*, September 23, 1873.
322. *Daily Shreveport Times*, October 2, 1873. Note here the use of the wording "his government" and "our people."
323. *Daily Shreveport Times*, October 2, 1873.
324. Ibid.; October 3, 1873; *New York Times*, September 26, 1873.
325. *Daily Shreveport Times*, October 2, 1873.

326. Ibid., October 4, 1873; October 5, 1873.
327. Ibid., October 2, 1873; October 5, 1873; October 11, 1873.
328. Ibid., October 4, 1873; Baudier Historical Collection.

God Help and Relieve Them

329. The epidemic of New Orleans in 1853 claimed approximately twelve thousand lives.
330. Nolan, *Splendors of Faith*, 46; Baudier Historical Collection; Biever, *Jesuits in New Orleans*, 95.
331. Baudier Historical Collection; *Daily Picayune*, October 4, 2018.
332. Archives of the Archdiocese of New Orleans.
333. *Daily Shreveport Times*, October 4, 1873.
334. Ibid., October 5, 1873; October 8, 1873; October 9, 1873.
335. Matthew 9:1–8, Gospel reading of the Eighteenth Sunday after Pentecost.
336. Correspondence of Mother Mary Hyacinth Le Conniat; Ignatius, *Across Three Centuries*, 284–85.
337. "So be it, so be it, so be it." Daughters of the Cross, "Victims of 1873 Yellow Fever Epidemic." It is clear from the letters of Mother Mary Hyacinth that precautionary administrations of Holy Viaticum were being offered in some gravely ill cases. It seems likely the novice Rose was able to receive the host, though the timeline of her death closely preceded the advent of Father LeVézouët's own illness.
338. *Daily Shreveport Times*, October 8, 1873.
339. Ibid.
340. Correspondence of James Muse Dabbs.
341. *Daily Shreveport Times*, October 8, 1873.
342. *Rapides Gazette*, October 25, 1873; correspondence of Bishop Auguste Martin.
343. Correspondence of Bishop Auguste Martin; *Daily Shreveport Times*, October 5, 1873; October 9, 1873; *New Orleans Times Picayune*, February 28, 1900.
344. Correspondence of Mother Mary Hyacinth Le Conniat; Sacramental Register of Holy Trinity Church, Shreveport, Louisiana.
345. *Daily Shreveport Times*, October 11, 1873.

Bring Along Their Coffins

346. *Daily Shreveport Times*, October 1, 1873.
347. Ibid.; October 9, 1873.
348. Ibid., October 10, 1873.
349. Ibid.
350. Ibid., October 9, 1873; October 10, 1873.
351. Ibid., October 11, 1873.
352. Ibid., October 12, 1873.
353. Psalms 91:15.
354. *Daily Shreveport Times*, October 15, 1873; October 16, 1873.
355. Ibid., October 15, 1873; October 17, 1873.
356. Hall, personal diary, October 6–7, 1873.
357. *Daily Shreveport Times*, October 15, 1873; Hall, personal diary, October 6–7, 1873.
358. *Daily Shreveport Times*, October 17, 1873.
359. United States Census, 1860; *Daily Shreveport Times*, October 19, 1873; *Holmes County Republican*, November 27, 1873.
360. *Daily Shreveport Times*, October 19, 1873; *Holmes County Republican*, November 27, 1873.
361. *Daily Shreveport Times*, October 21, 1873.
362. Letter from Bishop Auguste Martin to Father Joseph Gentille, October 14, 1873, Daughters of the Cross Collection, Noel Archives and Special Collections, Louisiana State University at Shreveport.
363. Ibid.
364. *Daily Shreveport Times*, October 21, 1873.
365. Ibid., October 22, 1873.
366. Ibid.
367. Ibid., October 21, 1873.
368. Ibid.
369. Ibid., October 23, 1873; October 24, 1873. This mortality rate is very high for yellow fever and calls into question the medical practices of the day.
370. Ibid., October 23, 1873.
371. Obituary of Father John James Duffo, SJ, *Woodstock Letters*, Jesuit Online Library.
372. *Daily Shreveport Times*, October 24, 1873.
373. Ibid.

Glad Tidings

374. Dumas and Deshusses, *Liber Sacramentorum Gellonensis.* This text dates to the eighth century.
375. *Daily Shreveport Times*, October 25, 1873; October 26, 1873.
376. Ibid., October 25, 1873; October 26, 1873.
377. Ibid., October 26, 1873.
378. Ibid.
379. Ibid.
380. Prayer based on Luke 4:38–44 and the Collect of *Missa in Tempore Mortalitatis.*
381. *Daily Shreveport Times*, October 29, 1873; October 30, 1873.
382. The *Aedes aegypti* mosquito is today understood to be an early morning and late afternoon to early evening feeder. Certainly, the physicians were cognizant of the smaller chances of becoming infected during the bright daylight hours.
383. *Daily Shreveport Times*, November 15, 1873.
384. Ibid., October 30, 1873.
385. Ibid., October 31, 1873.
386. Ibid., November 15, 1873.
387. Ibid., November 2, 1873.
388. Father Joseph Gentille, personal diary, Archives of the Diocese of Shreveport, Shreveport, Louisiana.
389. *Daily Picayune*, October 4, 1873.

All Honor to the Noble Martyrs

390. *Catholic News Messenger*, December 21, 1873.
391. Ibid.
392. *Daily Shreveport Times*, November 15, 1873.
393. Parish history of St. Matthew's Church.
394. Letter of Bishop Auguste Martin to Father Joseph Gentille; McCants, *They Came to Louisiana*, 226.
395. Sacramental Register, Holy Trinity Church.
396. Correspondence of Bishop Auguste Martin.
397. Plauché, *Brief History of Holy Trinity Church*, 32.
398. *Daily Shreveport Times*, November 7, 1873.
399. Correspondence of Bishop Auguste Martin.

400. Father Joseph Gentille, personal diary; *Daily Shreveport Times*, February 5, 1873; *Morning Star and Catholic News Messenger*, February 13, 1876.
401. Father Joseph Gentille, personal diary.
402. Ibid.
403. Ibid.
404. Ibid.
405. Ibid.
406. Correspondence of Bishop Auguste Martin.

Bibliography

Alabama Medical Association. *Transactions of the Medical Association of the State of Alabama*, Session 27, 1874.

Allen, Francis R. "Development of the Public Health Movement in the Southeast." *Social Forces* 22, no. 1 (1904).

American Association for the Advancement of Science. "Symposium on Yellow Fever and Other Insect Borne Diseases." *Science* 23, no. 58 (March 1906): 4.

———. "Yellow Fever and Mosquitoes." *Science* 12, no. 305 (November 1900).

American Catholic Historical Society. "Southern Historical Notes." *American Catholic Historical Researches*, New Series, 2, no. 2 (1906).

American Church Almanac and Yearbook: 1898–99. New York: James Pott and Company, 1911.

Archdiocese of New Orleans, Louisiana.

Archdiocese of Rennes, France.

Archdiocese of St. Louis, Missouri.

Baudier Historical Collection, vol. 23 (Heroes of '73). Archives of the Archdiocese of New Orleans.

Bell, A.N., ed. *The Sanitarian: A Monthly Magazine Dedicated to the Preservation of Health, Mental and Physical Culture*. Vol. 2 (1874).

Biever, Albert H. *The Jesuits in New Orleans and the Mississippi Valley: Jubilee Memorial*. New Orleans: Society of Jesus, 1924.

Blanc, Archbishop Antoine. Correspondence. Archives of the University of Notre Dame, South Bend, Indiana.

Booth, Augustine R. "An Inaugural Dissertation on History of the Epidemic of Shreveport, Louisiana." University of Kentucky Medical School, 1873.

Boston Medical and Surgical Journal, vol. 90.

Boyce, Robert William. *Yellow Fever and Its Prevention: A Manual for Medical Students and Practitioners*. New York: E.P. Dutton and Company, 1911.

Branche, Jerome C., ed. *Post Colonialism and the Pursuit of Freedom in the Black Atlantic*. New York: Routledge Publishers, 2018.

Breeden, James O. "Joseph Jones and Public Health in the New South." *Louisiana History: The Journal of the Louisiana Historical Association* 32, no. 4 (August 1991).

Brock, Eric J. *Shreveport*. Baton Rouge, LA: Pelican Publishing Company, 2001.

———. *Shreveport Chronicles: Profiles from Louisiana's Port City*. Charleston, SC: The History Press, 2009.

Butler, Father Alban. *Lives of the Saints*. New York: Tan Book Publishers, 1994.

Carrigan, JoAnn. *The Saffron Scourge: A History of Yellow Fever in Louisiana, 1796–1905*. Lafayette: University of Southwestern Louisiana Press, 1994.

Carroll, James, William C. Gorgas, Robert L. Owen and Walter D. McCaw. *Yellow Fever: A Compilation of Various Publications*. Washington, D.C.: United States Government Printing Office, 1911.

Carter, Henry Rose. *Yellow Fever: An Epidemiological and Historical Study of Its Place of Origin*. New York: Williams and Wilkins, 1931.

Catholic Encyclopedia. New York: Robert Appleton Company, 1917.

Catholic News Messenger (New Orleans, LA).

Catholic Propagator (New Orleans, LA).

Chaves-Carballo, Enrique. "Clara Maass, Yellow Fever, and Human Experimentation." *Military Medicine* (2013): 178.

Chicago Tribune.

Christophers, Sir S. Rickard. *Aedes Aegypti: The Yellow Fever Mosquito, Its Life History, Bionomics and Structure*. Cambridge, UK: Cambridge University Press, 1960.

The Clinic. Cincinnati, OH, January 10, 1874.

Coleman, William L. *A History of Yellow Fever: Indisputable Facts, Origin and Cause*. Chicago: Clinic Publishing Company, 1898.

Colonial Dames. *Historical Profile of Shreveport*. Shreveport, LA, 1850.

Crosby, Mary Caldwell. *The American Plague: The Untold Story of Yellow Fever, the Epidemic That Shaped Our History*. New York: Berkeley Books, 2006.

Dabbs, James Muse. Letters. Ouachita Parish Louisiana History. www.usgwarchives.net.

Daily Shreveport Times.

D'Antoni, Blaise G. "Bayou Pierre: Land of Yesteryear: A Sesquicentennial History of Immaculate Conception Chapel of Carmel and the Church of the Holy Apostles of Bayou Pierre, 1808–1958." Unpublished manuscript, Archives of the Diocese of Shreveport, Louisiana.

Daughters of the Cross. Register. Archives of the Diocese of Shreveport, Louisiana.

———. "Victims of 1873 Yellow Fever Epidemic. Shreveport, Louisiana." Unpublished manuscript. Archives of the Diocese of Shreveport, Louisiana.

Diocese of Alexandria, Louisiana, Archives.

Diocese of Nantes, France, Archives.

Diocese of Shreveport, Louisiana, Archives.

Diocese of St. Brieuc, France, Archives.

Doughty, Edward. *Observations and Inquiries into the Nature and Treatment of Yellow, or Bulam,* Fever. London, 1816.

Duffy, J. "Yellow Fever in the Continental United States in the Nineteenth Century." *Bulletin of the New York Academy of Medicine* 44 (June 1968).

Dumas, Antoine, and Jean Deshusses, eds. *Liber Sacramentorum Gellonensis.* Turnholti, Belgium, 1981.

Elford, Madeline. "A Brief History of St. Vincent's Academy and Daughters of the Cross." Unpublished manuscript, Archives of the Diocese of Shreveport, Louisiana.

Espinosa, Mariola. "The Question of Racial Immunity to Yellow Fever in History and Historiography." *Social Science History* 38, nos. 3–4 (Fall–Winter 2014).

Ford, W. Hutson. *Reports to the St. Louis Medical Society on Yellow Fever.* St. Louis, MO: George Rumbold and Company, 1878.

Frank Leslie's Illustrated Newspaper (New York).

Garvey, Joan B., and Mary Lou Widmer. *Beautiful Crescent: A History of New Orleans.* Gretna, LA: Pelican Publishing, 2013.

Gentille, Father Joseph. Personal diary. Archives of the Diocese of Shreveport, Louisiana.

Gergaud, Father Louis. Letters. Archives of the Diocese of Nantes, France.

———. Personal diary. Archives of St. Matthew's Church, Monroe, Louisiana.

Goodyear, James D. "The Sugar Connection: A New Perspective on the History of Yellow Fever." *Bulletin of the History of Medicine* 52, no. 1 (Spring 1978).

Grand Seminary of Nantes. Records. Archives of the Diocese of Nantes, France.

Gudmestad, Robert. *Steamboats and the Rise of the Cotton Kingdom*. Baton Rouge: Louisiana State University Press, 2011.

Hale, W. Chris, Gary D. Joiner, Bernadette Palombo and Cheryl H. White. *Wicked Shreveport*. Charleston, SC: The History Press, 2011.

Hall, Judge Henry Gerard. Personal diary. Noel Archives and Special Collections, Louisiana State University at Shreveport.

Hennessey, James. "The First Vatican Council." *Archivium Historiae Pontificiae* 7 (1969).

Hildreth, Peggy Bassett. "Early Red Cross: The Howard Association of New Orleans, 1837–1878." *Louisiana History: The Journal of the Louisiana Historical Association* 20, no. 1 (Winter 1979).

Hill, Ralph N. *The Doctors Who Conquered Yellow Fever*. New York: Random House, 1957.

Holmes County [OH] Republican.

Holy Trinity Church. Archives of the Diocese of Shreveport, Louisiana.

———. Sacramental Registers, Shreveport, Louisiana.

Howard Association. "Report of the Committee on the Yellow Fever Epidemic of 1873 at Shreveport, Louisiana." Shreveport, Louisiana, 1874.

Howard, Leland O. *Concerning the Geographic Distribution of the Yellow Fever Mosquito*. Washington, D.C.: United States Government Printing Office, 1902.

Humphreys, Margaret. *Yellow Fever and the South*. Baltimore, MD: Johns Hopkins University Press, 1992.

Ignatius, Sister Saint, DC. *Across Three Centuries*. New York: Benzinger Brothers, 1932.

Jefferson [TX] Democrat.

Johnson, Margaret. "The Great Yellow Fever Epidemic of Shreveport in 1873." *North Louisiana Historical Journal* 30, no. 4 (n.d.).

Joiner, Gary D., and Cheryl H. White. *Shreveport's Oakland Cemetery: Spirits of Pioneers and Heroes*. Charleston, SC: The History Press, 2015.

Joiner, Gary D., PhD. Professor and chair, Department of History, Louisiana State University at Shreveport. Personal interview.

Journal of the Telegraph (New York).

Kelly, Howard Atwood. *Walter Reed and Yellow Fever*. New York: McClure, Phillips, and Company: 1906.

Kotar, S.L., and J.E. Gessler. *Yellow Fever: A Worldwide History*. Jefferson, NC: McFarland and Company Publishing, 2017.

LaRoche, Rene. *Yellow Fever Considered in Its Historical, Pathological, Etiological, and Thermapeutical Relations*. Philadelphia: Blanchard and Lea Publishers, 1855.

Leavity, Judith W., and Ronald L. Numbers, eds. *Sickness and Health in America: Readings in the History of Medicine and Public Health*. Madison: University of Wisconsin Press, 1997.

Le Conniat, Mother Mary Hyacinth. Correspondence. Noel Archives and Special Collections, Louisiana State University at Shreveport.

Lining, John. *Description of the American Yellow Fever in the Year 1748*. Philadelphia, 1799.

Mahe, Reverend C. "History of the Missions of the Ouachita." Unpublished manuscript, 1929. Archives of the Archdiocese of New Orleans, Louisiana.

Martin, Bishop Auguste Marie. Annual Reports to the Society for the Propagation of the Faith, Paris, France. MPFP-096. Archives of the University of Notre Dame, South Bend, Indiana.

———. Correspondence to the Society for the Propagation of the Faith, Paris, France. MPFP-096. Archives of the University of Notre Dame, South Bend, Indiana.

———. Letters. Daughters of the Cross Collection, Noel Archives and Special Collections, Louisiana State University at Shreveport, Shreveport, Louisiana.

———. Letters. Register of the Daughters of the Cross, Archives of the Diocese of Shreveport, Louisiana.

———. "Notice on Very Rev. Father Gergaud from the Right Rev. Aug. Marie Martin, Bishop of Natchitoches." *Catholic Propagator*, November 12, 1873.

———. Personal diary (Vatican Council). Archives of the Archdiocese of New Orleans, Louisiana.

Martin, James W. *Yellow Fever: A Monograph*. Edinburgh, UK: Livingstone, 1892.

McCants, Sister Dorothea Olga. *They Came to Louisiana: Letters of a Catholic Mission, 1854–1882*. N.p.: Daughters of the Cross, 1983.

McLure, Mary Lilla, and Jolley Edward Howe. *History of Shreveport and Shreveport Builders*. Shreveport, LA: Journal Printing Company, 1937.

Miciotto, Robert J. "Shreveport's First Major Health Crisis: The Yellow Fever Epidemic of 1873." *North Louisiana Historical Journal* 4, no. 4 (n.d.).

Missale Romanum. Tours, France, 1869.

Nashville Union and American.

Natchitoches Parish, Louisiana: Conveyance Records. Natchitoches Parish Courthouse.

New Orleans Picayune.

New York Times.

New York World.

Nolan, Charles E. *Splendors of Faith: New Orleans Catholic Churches, 1727–1930.* Baton Rouge: Louisiana State University Press, 2010.

Nott, Josiah. "The Cause of Yellow Fever." *New Orleans Medical and Surgical Journal* 4 (1848).

Oldstone, Michael B. *Viruses, Plagues, and History.* Oxford, UK: Oxford University Press, 2000.

O'Pry, Maude Hearn. *Chronicles of Shreveport.* Shreveport, LA, 1928.

Ouachita Citizen (Monroe, LA).

Ouachita Telegraph (Monroe, LA).

Paine, Thomas. *Miscellaneous Letters and Essay on Various Subjects.* London, 1819.

Partain, Father Chad A. *A Tool Pushed by Providence: Bishop Auguste Martin and the Catholic Church in North Louisiana.* Austin, TX: Persidia Publishing, 2010.

Patterson, K. David. "Yellow Fever Epidemics and Mortality in the United States, 1693–1905." *Social Science and Medicine* 34, no. 8 (April 1992).

Pierce, John R., and James V. Writer. *Yellow Jack: How Yellow Fever Ravaged America and Walter Reed Discovered Its Deadly Secrets.* Hoboken, NJ: Wiley and Sons, 2005.

Plauche, Right Reverend Monsignor J.V. *A Brief History of Holy Trinity Church, Shreveport, Louisiana, and of the Catholic Church in Northwest Louisiana.* Shreveport, LA, 1942.

Radcliffe, J. "A Note on the Recurrence of Yellow Fever Epidemics in Urban Populations." *Journal of Applied Probability* 11, no. 1 (March 1974).

Rapides Gazette (Alexandria, LA).

Rawson, Reverend F.T. "Memorial of Father Louis Gergaud." *Ouachita Telegraph* (Monroe, LA), October 24, 1873.

"Report of the Committee on the Yellow Fever Epidemic of 1873 of Shreveport, Louisiana." *American Journal of the Medical Sciences* 66, no. 134 (1874).

Sadlier, D & J. *Sadlier's Catholic Directory, Almanac, and Ordo.* New York, 1873.

Sant Loup Parish Church Sacramental Register, Lanloup, France.

The Scholastic. "Priests Who Have Died at Shreveport." South Bend, IN: University of Notre Dame, 1873.

Scudder, John M., ed. *The Eclectic Medical Journal.* Cincinnati, OH, 1874.

Seminary of St. Brieuc-Treguier. Records. Diocese of St. Brieuc, France.

Shmaefsky, Brian. *Deadly Diseases and Epidemics: Yellow Fever.* New York: Chelsea House Publishing, 2010.

Shreveport [LA] Journal.

Slout, William. *En Route to the Great Eastern Circus.* Rockville, MD: Wildside Books, 2011.

St. Columba Church, Brelidy, France. Sacramental Registers.

St. Matthew's Church Archives, Monroe, Louisiana.

St. Nicholas Church, Heric, France. Sacramental Registers.

Sternberg, George M. *Report on the Etiology and Prevention of Yellow Fever.* Washington, D.C.: United States Government Printing Office, 1890.

Strode, George K. *Yellow Fever.* New York: McGraw Hill Publishers, 1951.

Taylor, Milton W. *Viruses and Man: A History of Interactions.* New York: Springer International Publishing, 2014.

Toner, J.M. *Contributions to the Study of Yellow Fever: A Paper Read Before the American Public Health Association in New York on the Natural History and Distribution of Yellow Fever in the United States.* New York, 1874.

Touatre, Just. *Yellow Fever: Clinical Notes.* New Orleans: New Orleans Medical and Surgical Journal Publishing, 1898.

Tyson, Carl Newton. *The Red River in Southwestern History.* Norman: University of Oklahoma Press, 1981.

United States Census. Washington, D.C.: United States Census Bureau.

Vital Records Registry, Heric, France.

Vital Records Registry, Lanloup, France.

Vital Records Registry, Pleine-Fourgeres, France.

Vital Records Registry, Plourivo, France.

Warner, Margaret. "Hunting the Yellow Fever Germ: The Principle and Practice of Etiological Proof in Late Nineteenth Century America." *Bulletin of the History of Medicine* 59, no. 3 (Fall 1985).

Wills, Christopher. *Yellow Fever, Black Goddess: The Co-Evolution of People and Plagues.* Cambridge, MA: Perseus Publishing, 1996.

Woodruff, Lieutenant Eugene Augustus. Personal letter of September 9, 1873. Noel Archives and Special Collections, Louisiana State University at Shreveport.

Woodworth, John. *Annual Report of the Supervising Surgeon of the Marine Hospital Service of the United States for Fiscal Year 1874.* Washington, D.C.: United States Government Printing Office, 1974.

About the Authors

VERY REVEREND PETER B. MANGUM was raised in Shreveport, the oldest of five sons, parishioner of St. Jude Church in Bossier City and graduate of Christ the King School in Bossier City and Jesuit High School (now Loyola) in Shreveport. He attended Holy Trinity Seminary at the University of Dallas and then the Pontifical Gregorian University in Rome, where he remained for five years, receiving degrees in sacred theology and canon law, and making numerous pilgrimages to the shrines and tombs of saints in Rome and throughout Europe. Ordained a priest in 1990, "Father Peter" has served as the judicial vicar of the Diocese of Shreveport since 1993 and has served in various parishes before becoming rector of the parish and school of the Cathedral of St. John Berchmans in 2005. He served as chaplain of Loyola College Prep and is now also the director of vocations for the diocese. He has researched and actively promoted the causes of the five priests who died in Shreveport's yellow fever epidemic of 1873. In his capacity as diocesan administrator of Shreveport, he led a Shreveport delegation to Brittany, France, to the native dioceses and villages of the Shreveport Five, as well as visited twice the Congregation for the Causes of the Saints at the Vatican to learn more of the process of canonization as it applies to those who freely offered their lives and heroically accepted, out of Christian charity, a certain and untimely death.

W. RYAN SMITH is a native of Shreveport. A husband and father of three, he serves as the director of hospital operations at Ochsner LSU Health Shreveport, the contemporary descendant of the city's first charity hospital that was established as a direct result of the 1873 yellow fever epidemic. He worked with his staff throughout the COVID-19 pandemic, coordinating higher level of care hospital transfers, inpatient capacity management operations and outpatient COVID-19 vaccine scheduling for the region. He holds both a master of arts and a bachelor of business degree from Northwestern State University of Louisiana in Natchitoches, Louisiana, and has completed postgraduate work with both the Pennsylvania State University and Villanova University. He makes his home in Shreveport and became alerted to the story of the five priests while researching the medical history of the city of Shreveport. He has served on the board of Catholic Charities of North Louisiana, is a Knight of the Equestrian Order of the Holy Sepulchre of Jerusalem (a nearly one-thousand-year-old chivalrous order) and was named one of the Greater Shreveport Chamber's Young Professional Initiative's "40 under 40" in 2018. He is a parishioner of the Cathedral of St. John Berchmans in Shreveport. Smith is the author of *Sang pour Sang*, a novel published by the University of Louisiana at Lafayette Press (2018), and coauthor of *A Haunted History of Louisiana Plantations* (2017, The History Press), a work completed along with friend and fellow researcher Dr. Cheryl H. White.

Cheryl H. White, PhD, is a professor of history at Louisiana State University at Shreveport, where she has taught medieval European and Christian church history for twenty-five years. Dr. White currently holds the distinguished Hubert Humphreys Endowed Professorship, which has provided many research opportunities involving the field of Christian history, resulting in numerous peer-reviewed articles and professional academic conference presentations. A passionate preservationist, she is actively engaged in historic preservation advocacy and policy-making at both the local and state levels. As a native of northwest Louisiana, Dr. White's deep love of history was first nurtured in the rich narratives of her own home state, meaning that her research has been equally focused on stories much closer to home, many of which have been published in books and articles on regional history and folklore. It was the nexus of local history and Christian history that shaped her interest and collaboration in the extensive research on the five Shreveport martyr priests of 1873, shared with colleagues Father Peter Mangum and W. Ryan Smith. This is her sixth book to be published with The History Press.

Visit us at
www.historypress.com